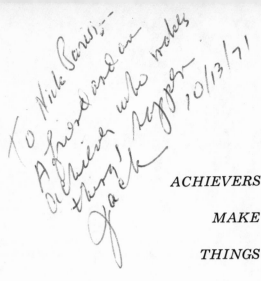

ACHIEVERS

MAKE

THINGS

HAPPEN

ACHIEVERS

MAKE

THINGS

HAPPEN

JACK H. GROSSMAN, Ph.D.
DePaul University
Director, Interpersonal Relations Institute

with
Sammye Malosky Johnson

Publishers/WHITEHALL COMPANY
601 Skokie Blvd./Northbrook, Ill.

Copyright © 1971 By

WHITEHALL COMPANY
601 Skokie Blvd./Northbrook, Ill.

Manufactured in the United States of America

SBN 0-87655-027-8

I respectfully dedicate this book to my friend, partner and wife, Joan, without whose encouragement this book could not have been written. And, to my children Lynn, Gayle, Michael and Gary, who are constant reminders of why I must continue to achieve; thank you for just being.

JHG

PREFACE

As is true with most books on human behavior, this one evolved through years of experience, research and observations. My serious interest in this subject began while I was a graduate student. At that time I did considerable reading on the subject of achievement and motivation, and chose to do my doctoral dissertation on this topic. My investigation dealt with "Personality and other nonacademic characteristics of bright underachieving high school males." In this study I identified certain self-defeating behaviors and attitudes which interfered with these students' productivity.

Later, when I taught at the university level, I found that these same qualities were also common to many college students. As a practicing psychologist I have encountered similar characteristics among many bright adults, both men and women. I recall one of the first talks I gave on this subject. It was before a middle management group. A participant said to me after my presentation, "It's like listening to a physician describe a disease, and discovering you've got it." Since that first talk, others have made similar comments to me.

Based upon these observations, I was convinced that the problems I had been discussing, and which are presented in this book, are universal. Age or sex is not a factor. Furthermore, judging from my experiences in dealing with these behaviors and attitudes, I am confident that the ideas and suggestions presented within these pages work. But you, and only you, can make them work. These are not magical formulas.

We are living in a fast moving society where people are continually searching for meaning to their lives, and for ways of utilizing their potential. While the restlessness and desire are there, many do not get past this stage. Some make halfhearted attempts, but fail to follow through. And others, perhaps the more ambitious, work toward their objectives, but they battle themselves in the process.

It is the aim of this book to provide the reader with a better understanding of himself, as well as some guidelines for overcoming his difficulties so that he can make things happen.

JHG

TABLE OF CONTENTS

ACHIEVERS

MAKE

THINGS

HAPPEN

CHAPTER I

ARE YOU MAKING THINGS HAPPEN?

You know the underachiever. He's the fellow who goes around with his eyes open and his mouth shut—except when he is making promises he can't keep or bragging about pseudo accomplishments. The underachiever can be either male or female, black or white, young or old. His face doesn't matter, for he's basically a nice fellow, the average guy at the office or at school who manages to plug in, but never really connects. He has chosen to sit on his potential, rather than try to fulfill it.

Take Steve, for example. At 35, he seems to be a fairly successful middle echelon businessman. He makes $15,000 a year as a salesman, and gives the impression of being a very independent operator.

Unfortunately, for both Steve and his company, his territory could yield him $30,000 a year. But because Steve is terrified of being rejected by clients, he makes it a point to call only on customers he thinks are sure accounts. If a prospective customer shows the slightest bit of hesitancy or resistance, he won't bother to make a second call. Steve's excuse is that "they won't buy anyway, so why waste time with them?"

His fear of failure causes him to withdraw from competition and he lacks the desire to put forth the necessary effort to succeed. He approaches every situation with a great deal of trepidation. Since he's already convinced that he won't make the sale, Steve is less than enthusiastic in his approach. This negative attitude comes through to customers, who naturally reject him. Steve may end up without a sale, but then, he wasn't expecting one anyway.

Others are like Betty, who cannot finish knitting a sweater, much less complete an advertising campaign for her long suffering boss. Though she has a well-paying job as a copyrighter, 29-year-old Betty still isn't sure what she wants to be when she grows up. She fantasizes a lot (the Cinderella story is her favorite daydream), but she has no real objective in life.

Betty has a "what's the use" attitude. She is capable of creating brilliant slogans and writing imaginative descriptions about soap, soup, and sex, but she is positive that no one is going to like her work. In fact, Betty is certain that her account supervisor will redo the entire project and label her a failure. So she does an inadequate, haphazard job and makes a lot of excuses.

Why is Betty so lacking in self-confidence? The answer lies in her childhood relationship with her mother. As a child Betty tried very hard to please her mother by washing the dishes, cleaning the house and ironing clothes. But no matter what she did, Mommy always found fault. And Mommy would do the dishes, the house and the clothes all over again.

So Betty grew up with the feeling that she couldn't do anything right. It didn't take her long to decide that the safest way was the way of least activity. "Besides," Betty reasons, "my boss will do it over . . . just as my mother did."

Most people want to be productive in their work so they can have a sense of accomplishment and realize their dreams. Those who are successful in fulfilling their goals are achievers. They make things happen; they welcome competition and always try to do their best.

Unfortunately, there are many people, equally as capable as achievers who sit on their potential rather than activate it. They spend half their lives wishing or waiting for success to come their way. But they do little to make their dreams come true. In fact, like Steve and Betty, their behavioral and attitudinal patterns are self-defeating.

Everyone underachieves to some extent. Seldom does a person utilize his full potential because we all have greater inner resources than can be tapped in a lifetime. The fact that successful people in one field are able to find new challenges, new talents to develop and ideas to probe, strongly suggests that we have a reservoir of untapped abilities.

Yet, many people do not even minimally utilize their abilities or their potential. These are the underachievers—the people who lack persistence and scatter their energies rather than direct their lives toward a specific goal. They have a tendency to focus on the emotional turmoil of a situation rather than face up to its challenge. They have a fear of failure which makes them unwilling to accept responsiblity or competition.

Sometimes they deny that they have any shortcomings and try to maintain a superior self-image. They create inordinately high standards and believe that they should achieve success with little effort. When they don't, they play the role of the suffering hero, become withdrawn or blame others for their difficulties, mistakes and failures.

On tests, they generally score high on ability. In fact, one sign of an underachiever is that his abilities far exceed his performance as judged by superiors or by himself. Because he dissipates his talents, he is a source of concern to those associated with him. No one likes to see talent wasted, including the person himself.

Why, then, will a Steve or a Betty continue to behave in the same damaging manner? A partial answer was given to me by a bright, 28-year-old chemist who, despite his capabilities and academic credentials, was at a career standstill: "My lack of success and inability to make of life what I want, makes me feel depressed, angry, frustrated, cynical toward people, bitter, and guilty that I'm not going anywhere. But my prevailing sense of helplessness is what scares me most."

His last sentence is a desperate cry for help. He really wants to achieve but he neither understands the nature of his difficulties nor does he know what to do about them. His problem is a common one.

Like the chemist, most underachievers know they are bright. They've been told many times, "If you weren't so lazy, you'd really get ahead"; "How can you be so bright yet act so dumb?"; "You have the ability to do better, why don't you?"

These familiar accusations simply do not work on an already bruised and highly sensitive ego. Nor do such punitive measures as scolding, threatening or firing do much to get an underachiever off his potential. Even more constructive approaches like increasing his responsibilities or pleading with him to do a better job fail to be successful for a significant period of time.

The notions that such an individual is lazy or that he doesn't care about his future are not completely valid. The truth is that many are unhappy with themselves because they realize that their halfhearted efforts to achieve are not getting them very far in their jobs or in their personal lives.

Ask these questions of yourself. Do you have difficulty making decisions? Do you have a tendency to procrastinate, putting things off until sometimes you even forget about doing them? Do you become easily upset if someone criticizes your work? Do you worry about what other people think about you?

These are all characteristics that interfere with your growth. You may not show these symptoms all the time. But, anyone can be a situational underachiever—performing less than he is capable in a certain job or certain environment.

I used to be an underachiever myself. I did poorly in grammar school, so poorly in fact that I was told I should go to a trade high school. But since I had no mechanical ability, I went on to a regular high school where I made mostly C's and D's in my courses. Part of the reason for this was that I didn't want to do the things you had to do to pass a course in school. Yet, I was bright enough to place first in a national English examination even though I was flunking junior English.

I hated high school and wanted to get out of it as soon as I could. So in my junior year I took an examination whereby

I could be admitted to the University of Chicago at the end of my junior year. The admissions officers told me I did well, that they'd like to have me, and to send a transcript. After I sent my transcript, which was atrocious, that was the end of that.

Just before I graduated from high school (in the lower half of my class) my counselor told me not to bother about going to college because I'd never make it. I was told to go to a trade school or get a job.

Instead, I went to a branch university near home and just barely got by with a C average. In fact, I didn't start doing well at college until I met my wife during my junior year. She bolstered my ego, telling me that I was capable of achieving. So I did.

Previously everyone seemed to tell me, "You'll never amount to anything. You're not capable of making it. So why try?"

The self-fulfilling prophecy being what it is, I wouldn't do as well as I could have. When I met my wife, she prophesized something else. She said that I was capable of being successful.

Though my grades improved in my junior and senior years, I only had a C average when I graduated. I had a difficult time being accepted at graduate school. I'll never forget what the chairman of one psychology department told me: "You just don't have what it takes to make it. You need verbal skills and you don't have them. You need analytic skills and you don't have them either. Why don't you get a job in business somewhere?"

However, the faith that a professor at Loyola University in Chicago had in me changed my destiny. As a result of the opportunity he gave me, I did exceedingly well and went on to earn my master of arts degree and my doctorate in psychology.

I had a lot of blows and I know that an underachiever will use his setbacks as an excuse for continuing to be an underachiever: "See, everybody says I'm no good. So why bother?" But the achiever says he doesn't care what anybody says; he's going to do it anyway.

The point is, you can overcome self-defeating habits and attitudes, and learn how to achieve rather than continuing to underperform. You can learn to overcome the emotional and psychological reasons for your tendency to underachieve. And if you are an occasional underachiever (and we all are), you can improve your work patterns and become even more successful in your life.

Types of Underachievers

There are two types of underachievers: the situational and the chronic. Situational underachievers are people who exhibit self-defeating behaviors under certain conditions only. At other times they do what is required to achieve. In other words, if they have a job which is not appealing to them, their actions and attitudes are such as to guarantee them failure. Yet, these same people perform extremely well when they are doing work which appeals to them.

For example, I sometimes find myself in a situation where I don't like what I'm doing. Bookkeeping particularly irritates me, and when I'm faced with that chore I will keep putting it off. I find other jobs to do which I think should be done first or I'll make excuses about not having the time to spend over the books. These are typical underachiever characteristics: procrastinating, working a little at a time, not really completing it, not being thorough with it.

So I have to stop myself and say, "Wait a minute. It's never going to get done this way. No one else will do the bookkeeping for you. You might as well get going so you can move on to jobs which you enjoy doing." It's a case of making a conscious effort to overcome a distasteful situation.

Most situational underachievers will manage to overcome this type of problem. But, when an underachieving individual falls into a job situation that he doesn't like, he can get so hung up on job security and fringe benefits that he won't do the best job. Instead, he will do only an okay job because he feels stuck.

Sometimes an initially interesting job will become boring for a person and cause him to act like an underachiever. Take the case of Elaine, who was valedictorian of her high school class, elected to Phi Beta Kappa in college, and received a bachelor of arts degree in mathematics. She was doing a good job as a sophisticated programmer for about a year, when suddenly her supervisor noticed a definite decline in her performance and interest in work. His attempts to reverse this poor motivational trend by talking with her, giving her an increase in salary and sending her to a week long training program failed.

This was a clear case of a situational underachiever. When I saw Elaine I merely posed one question, "Do you like your job as well as you did when you started?"

"No, I don't," Elaine replied. "It isn't challenging because I've been doing a lot of routine programming that anyone with less training could do. Because we're understaffed, I'm stuck with it."

Once her supervisor was told what the source of the problem was, he restructured her work. Within a week she became enthusiastic again and began to produce. Thus, when the situation improved, Elaine's work output and attitude also changed for the better.

The chronic underachievers are those who function beneath their potential in almost any intellectually demanding situation which they encounter. They also do poorly in any task which requires concentration and self-discipline. For them poor performance and a negativistic attitude is a way of life—a habit pattern which is reflected in their work, as well as in their personal lives.

Many people fall into the underachieving trap because they have a fear of failure. They are afraid of trying because if an all-out effort did not produce the results they expected, they wouldn't have an excuse to use. John, an engineer, was assigned a rather complex project for which he had full responsibility. Six months later the project was still in the rough, rough draft stage. Investigation revealed that John did not fully understand what needed to be done. He was too embarrassed to ask, so he did a minimal job. He felt it was safer to just get by and be labeled as "lazy" than to put himself to the test, gather all the pertinent material, and take the risk of failing.

It is interesting to note that situational underachievers, when they are working in an environment that is unsuitable or unchallenging to them, exhibit almost the same characteristics as the chronic type. They are just as motivationally paralyzed. So, for all practical purposes it doesn't matter with which label you identify. If you feel you can make more things happen, you can benefit from this book.

The Underachiever's Dilemma

If one phrase could be used to describe these highly complex and potentially productive individuals it would be that they are "a ball of self-contradictions." They are constantly fighting themselves. They want to achieve but they do not want to put forth the required effort. They want to get ahead in their careers but they have no plan of action for realizing their objectives. They want to be independent yet they have a strong need to please those in authority. They set goals and objectives they cannot possibly reach. In short, their desires are inconsistent with or in opposition to their actions.

As a result of these inner conflicts they have a confused self-concept. They are continuously frustrated and trapped between what they think they can do and what they really are able to do. Their inability to get out of this self-created box causes them to become suspicious and fearful of others. Some resign themselves to their condition by assuming they are born losers or jinxed. Others desperately try to overcome their obstacles by promising to do better. They make elaborate resolutions to be more productive. But their verbal determinations are rarely converted into action.

Paul, for example, has learned that he can create a good impression at work with his supervisors by talking about forthcoming campaigns from his promotion department staff. As assistant chief of sales promotion, Paul is responsible for finding new ways of advertising the firm's products and services. Unfortunately for Paul, when he is asked to produce his latest inspiration, he must hedge and make excuses about staff slowdowns. He talks about how productive he is and how much he contributes to the final outcome. Sometimes Paul even believes he is the department's mainstay. But he's been passed over for promotion twice.

Many begin showing this behavior during their early school years, revealing the pattern in poor academic performance despite the fact that tests show average or above average intelligence. Even if they are bright enough to get by in school their attitudes will catch up with them in the nonprotective environment of work.

Alex, a young commercial artist, is unable to keep up with the job pace and puts in considerably more hours than the job actually requires. Alex does well financially, but has uneasy feelings about his success.

"I keep feeling that I'm riding a bubble instead of a solid foundation," Alex told me. "I don't really deserve the money I'm getting. I feel someday I will be found out and the bubble will burst."

His concern was legitimate. Alex's work pattern and attitude were such that his effectiveness as an artist was considerably reduced. Just as he anticipated, one day the agency discovered his inability to work on a tight daily deadline and fired him.

Once a self-defeating pattern is established, mediocrity becomes the way of life. An inventory of excuses becomes one's best friend. Blaming the teacher, the school, the job, the supervisor is better than blaming yourself. And you hope that excuses which justify your inactivity (not enough time, not enough material) will appease those who want to know why you aren't doing better.

Self-deceptions like: "I am lazy" or "If I really tried, I could do better" or "I don't have the right connections" cease to be consoling when you are making little progress. David used all of these excuses when he was in school. But not receiving good grades in school is a small price to pay compared to being skipped over for promotions, failing to advance financially and having no sense of direction or feeling of accomplishment.

After 10 years as an insurance underwriter, David began to sense that he was at a career standstill. He even doubted the validity of some of his excuses when his boss and his family began to lose patience with him. He was ignored at home by his family and not consulted on the most basic policies at the office. Though he finally saw that there is no substitute for action and results, he didn't know what to do about his dilemma. David ended up disliking himself; he became hopelessly depressed and lost his grip on the few ambitions he did have at one time.

It is not easy to break ingrained habits and attitudes which have served a useful purpose for a long time—avoiding responsibilities that require self-discipline. But it can be done. What is required is a conscious and planned approach, as well as an understanding of the factors that prevent achievement.

Only a deliberate and rational plan of attack can replace nonproductive habit patterns with result-producing habits. In short, everyone can learn to achieve.

Taking Inventory

Is it hard for you to give an opinion even when you know what you want to say? When a decision you've made is questioned, do you become filled with doubts and go into long apologetic explanations? Do you fantasize a lot?

To help you identify the specific behaviors and attitudes which may have been interfering with your development as a successful person, complete the following inventory. You might as well be completely candid since no one but you will see your answers.

Instructions: For each of the statements, indicate the degree to which it applies to you. Use the following point scale as your guide and place the appropriate number in the parenthesis provided:

5. Describes me perfectly

4. Almost always applies to me

3. Sometimes applies to me

2. Rarely applies to me

1. Never applies to me

The Behavioral and Attitudinal Inventory

(   )   1. I am very disorganized.

(   )   2. I tend to underestimate the amount of effort or time it takes to do a really good job.

(   )   3. I want to do better, and feel I can, but I don't know how.

(   )   4. I have difficulties making decisions about what needs to be done next.

(   )   5. I tend to look for the easy way out whenever possible.

(   )   6. I wait until the last possible moment to get started on difficult tasks which require my attention.

(   )   7. I rarely put forth my best effort at work.

(   )   8. Even when I work hard, I don't seem to make much headway.

(   )   9. I spend more time thinking about what I should do than actually doing things.

(   )   10. If a task requires a great deal of effort, I tend to put it off; sometimes I even forget about it.

(   )   11. When I am reading my mind tends to wander; I have difficulties concentrating.

(   )   12. I have wishes or daydreams of being ill or incapacitated.

(   )   13. I complain a great deal about how difficult things are for me.

( ) 14. I am afraid of failing at difficult tasks or when entering competition.

( ) 15. I seem to be under constant pressure.

( ) 16. I am afraid of too much responsibility.

( ) 17. I seem to be preoccupied with my problems, and think about them almost constantly.

( ) 18. Although others may not know it, I really lack confidence in my abilities.

( ) 19. I have difficulties making major decisions.

( ) 20. I am displeased with myself.

( ) 21. I don't like to check over my own work; I prefer someone else do it.

( ) 22. I do not admit, either to myself or others, that I have shortcomings; I feel I *should be* perfect.

( ) 23. At work, when I'm not sure about what has to be done, I stew about it rather than ask questions.

( ) 24. My desire to be perfect at things I do slows me down.

( ) 25. If I can't be one of the best at something my tendency is to quit or give up.

( ) 26. What others think of my work is generally more important to me than what I think of it.

( ) 27. When I do not succeed at a task I tend to blame others for it, or find fault in factors outside of me; it's usually someone else's fault.

( ) 28. I set *impossible* standards for myself.

( ) 29. My career goals are unclear; I do not know toward what career my efforts are leading me.

( ) 30. I do not develop plans for accomplishing long range objectives.

( ) 31. I do a great deal of wishing for things to happen, but have difficulties taking appropriate steps.

( ) 32. I tend to have a defeatist "what's the use" attitude.

( ) 33. I am concerned that if I really did well, and succeeded, people would expect me to maintain that pace constantly; and I may not be able to deliver.

( ) 34. I feel I should be able to accomplish difficult tasks with minimum amount of effort.

( ) 35. I tend to be enthusiastic when I begin an activity, but lose interest when I run into difficulties.

( ) 36. I start many projects or activities, but I tend not to follow through on most.

( ) 37. The goals I set for myself are seemingly out of reach.

( ) 38. I want to do many things but I don't like to take time to learn how.

( ) 39. When I have a project to do, I do not plan a course of action; my tendency is to dive in.

( ) 40. I become upset *easily* when my work is criticized or its quality is questioned, even if the criticism is logical and well explained.

(　) 41. I seem to be overly concerned with myself and the impression I make on others.

(　) 42. I generally have difficulties taking orders.

(　) 43. I feel I need more encouragement than most people.

(　) 44. I usually need, although I don't like it, prodding or outside pressures to get me going on a task or project.

(　) 45. I lose interest in people who do not pay attention to me.

(　) 46. If I really like a boss I will work extra hard for him, but I'll just do the minimum to get by if I don't like that person.

(　) 47. I make all kinds of promises to people, even though I can't deliver.

(　) 48. I worry a great deal about what others think of me.

(　) 49. Most bosses don't really understand me or appreciate my true abilities.

(　) 50. It is important that everyone like me.

(　) 51. I feel most bosses really don't know what they're doing.

(　) 52. I tend to be confused about what others expect from me and what I want from myself.

(　) 53. I want the opinion of others, yet I am afraid of what they will say.

How to Interpret the Inventory

Although most chronic underachievers will respond with a "4" or "5" on more than ninety per cent of the items, your total score or the label you give yourself is unimportant. (That's what makes this test different from others you may have taken.) Rather than adding up your score, go back and circle each of the items which either describe you perfectly (5) or almost always apply to you (4). These are the characteristics which have probably caused you to underachieve and therefore require your attention.

Even if one or two of the test items are descriptive of you, if they have been a source of difficulty or have interfered with your progress, you owe it to yourself to consider changing. The fact is that many successful people have some traits of an underachieving personality which work against them.

Let's say, for example, that item one (I am very disorganized) almost always applies to you. Even though this may be the only characteristic which describes you, if you fail to correct it you are needlessly stunting your rate of progress. You are not meeting your potential all the way.

Those traits that you marked as "3," while not crucial, should be reexamined with the aim of reducing their frequency of occurrence. If you truly wish to become an achiever, your objective should be to do away with as many self-defeating behaviors as possible.

CHAPTER II

FACTORS THAT INFLUENCE YOUR
SELF-CONCEPT

Importance and Origin of Self-Concept

How do you see yourself? Do you think you're a swinger or
do you prefer to be considered a conservative member of the
establishment? Do you think you're an intellectual or an
activist? Do you try to be debonair, with just a touch of the
avant garde in your clothes, your speech and your ideas?
Are you dainty and feminine or vigorous and masculine? Do
you make an impression on people you meet because you're
dynamic and dashing?

Or is the entire subject of image fuzzy and one which you
would prefer not to discuss because you have a tendency to
fade into the wallpaper or be lost in a cocktail crowd between
the hors d'oeuvres and the napkins? Can you even describe
yourself in positive, glowing terms? Or do you describe yourself as a person who prefers not to make any impression
at all?

What a person thinks about himself has a bearing on his
actions and on his work performance. If you sincerely believe
you are capable, bright and able to meet challenges, your
actions will reflect this image of yourself. On the other hand,
if you believe that you do not have these qualities you will
present an image which supports this notion.

For these reasons it is easy to see why an individual who
has an unfavorable image of himself will unconsciously seek

failure. In effect he is saying to himself, "I am not worthy or capable of succeeding, so why bother?" So he doesn't bother and he fails. Conversely, the person who values himself and his abilities will succeed because he wants to maintain this positive impression of himself.

Many people have a confused self-concept. On one hand they try to give the impression that they are self-sufficient and capable of performing Herculean tasks with a minimum of effort. Yet, in reality, they lack confidence in themselves and feel inadequate. They generally resolve this inconsistency by avoiding situations which would reveal their true feelings. Their excuse is, "I'm lazy" or "I don't have time" when what they really mean is "I'm afraid of trying."

How does an individual develop his self-concept? What factors influence you to view yourself in favorable or unfavorable ways?

Probably the single most important factor is past experience. If you are told repeatedly by those you respect or consider important—parents, other relatives, friends, teachers, bosses—that you are no good and never will amount to anything, the easy way out is to prove them right.

I recall listening to a group of five young rehabilitated ex-convicts tell an audience about the circumstances which led them into crime. The underlying theme of each participant's story was this: "As long as I can remember, no one had much faith in me. My parents thought I was a bum; my teachers thought I was stupid; the people I worked for treated me like a second class citizen. Even when I did good work and tried to be decent, no one paid much attention to me. They thought it was just a coincidence. I began to believe that maybe I was all those bad things. So I thought if I couldn't do anything right and if I was going to be treated as a delinquent, why not go all the way? That's when I started to get into trouble. I developed delinquent attitudes and created the conditions to maintain the unfavorable image I had of myself..

When I asked the participants what caused them to seek a more productive way of life, the theme that emerged was this:

"Someone (warden, social worker, psychologist) expressed confidence in me. He led me to believe that I have what it takes to lead a good life without hurting others or destroying myself. He made me feel that I was basically a good person. And more important, he showed me how I could lead a better life. Because I believed this person, I began to realize that I did have more to offer than I originally thought."

By altering their image of themselves, each of these young men was able to direct his energies toward constructive ends. All five were either working at or pursuing a socially acceptable and personally satisfying trade or occupation.

While this example is extreme, many capable, but moderately productive people share similar past experiences. Those I have met either professionally or socially generally come from these types of homes: the overprotective, the overdemanding, the inconsistent or the indifferent.

Overprotective Parents

The overprotective home is one in which parents make few, if any, demands on their children. Such parents constantly indulge their youngsters and expect great things from them, but seldom allow them to make independent decisions. These children are also not allowed to learn from their mistakes because they are not permitted the luxury and freedom to venture into activities which may prove risky. Such parents insist on holding their child's hand regardless of how old he is. It is as if the parents are saying to their children, "I neither trust you to solve your own problems, nor do I want you to get hurt trying."

People who come from overprotective homes do not learn self-discipline. They learn instead that mother or dad (in later years, bosses and other authority figures) will come to their rescue if they don't pull through a task or assignment. Because they are treated as babies at home they fail to mature emotionally when they are on their own. It's no wonder that such individuals lack confidence in their abilities or judgments.

After all, how can you believe you are able to deal with problems if you haven't had the opportunity to do so?

This overprotectiveness is most often seen in the mother-daughter relationship. Some mothers won't let their daughters do anything by themselves. If Nancy is practicing the piano, Mommy is right there telling her which notes to hit. If Nancy tries a new hairdo, Mommy has several suggestions about how it could be done more attractively. Nancy is never allowed to do anything by herself so after a while she doesn't even bother to try. She feels ineffectual and incapable of meeting Mommy's expectations.

Another ploy used by mothers is an overprotective kind of one-upmanship. Carol knits a muffler for Daddy—Mommy designs and makes him a new shirt. Carol fixes a steak dinner one night—Mother turns out lobster and baked alaska the next evening. In this case, Mother is constantly saying, "I'm better." Eventually Carol believes it and concludes that she might as well do nothing.

Children from these backgrounds do not learn to develop confidence in themselves because they never learn to success-fully overcome obstacles. If obstacles are removed by other people, you learn to depend on them, rather than on your own inner resources. In effect you learn not to trust your-self because others do not trust you enough to let you try.

While many overprotective parents do not make demands on their children, they nonetheless expect big things from them. They will reward the child for his brightness but will not acknowledge his effort. This is inconsistent since achieve-ment requires discipline, hard work and a willingness to en-dure whatever hardships are necessary to succeed. Because children reared by such parents do not realize this, they develop an inflated and unrealistic self-esteem, self-decep-tiveness and they avoid challenges. They develop the notion that ability alone is enough to succeed and that success comes from luck and other magical ways. So we get the situation of a person who is bright and who expects to get promotions and to achieve financial stability without per-forming. Unfortunately for him, today's society rewards a person for performance rather than brightness.

The first child in a family is often told how bright and capable he is. He may be intelligent enough to do well during his first few years of school, but without exerting much effort. Billy is such a child. His parents were so proud that he knew the alphabet and his address before he went to kindergarten that they were always praising him. But the further Billy goes in school, the greater are the demands upon him.

Now he's in the seventh grade and he has this attitude toward homework: "I'm smart. I don't have to do this boring assignment." Billy's grades are beginning to drop; he is getting B's and C's when he should be getting A's.

Fortunately, Billy's parents realize that they have failed to teach him that brightness doesn't really matter if performance doesn't follow. So they are trying to undo Billy's self-defeating attitudes before it's too late. Now they try to overemphasize that performance counts. When Billy brags about how smart he is, his parents reply, "If you are so smart, why don't you make superior grades?" When this logical approach doesn't work, Billy's parents ask him if he is enjoying school.

Not surprisingly, Billy says he doesn't like school. So his parents point out that the only way he is going to get some enjoyment out of school is to do the assignments and try to get permission to try more creative and innovative extra credit work. This combination of positive reinforcement and encouragement is beginning to work.

Sometimes I counsel people from wealthy backgrounds who tell me, "My parents always gave me everything. They never made any demands on me." One fellow named Mark told me that he never had any guidelines as a child. His father had died when he was 3 years old and his mother overcompensated for it by never setting any limits for him.

Consequently, Mark simply drifted for years. Even in his position as a junior executive he drifted. He felt very unhappy with himself because he believed that he could accomplish things without expending much effort. But he didn't seem to make the money he could have with his educational background.

The company Mark worked for noticed his attitude and sent him to me for counseling. I asked him, "What do you want to do at your company?"

"I want to be vice president of purchasing," Mark replied.

"That's very good. Would you like to work in the purchasing department?"

"No, I don't like purchasing," Mark said.

"How are you going to become vice president of purchasing if you don't go through the purchasing department?"

"I don't know what I want to go through. All I know is that I want to be an executive."

"Fine. What route do you want to take?" I asked him.

"Well, I never thought about it."

It's this kind of feeling that's instilled by overprotective parents—that you can do anything you want and you can have any great position. But these parents fail to give you a direction or route to take. They don't mention that you have to work to achieve.

Overdemanding Parents

Those who come from overly demanding homes describe their parents as hypercritical. Such parents rarely encourage or compliment youngsters for their good performance because they expect their children to do well. But these parents are the first to criticize poor performance. Rarely do children from this kind of home do anything that is quite good enough. Invariably they fall short of their parents' unrealistically high standards.

Because the parents pay attention only to the child's failures, ignoring his successes, the contact between the parent and the child is through failure. The typical comment of individuals from overdemanding homes goes like this: "If I got an 'A' in a course at school, my parents didn't say anything. Of course I was bright, so what's the fuss? But if I didn't do well, they gave me all kinds of hell."

What happens to a child in this situation is psychologically shattering. He is taught to believe that no matter what effort he puts forth, it will be rejected or unacceptable. The only way for the child to maintain contact with his parents is to also see himself as a failure, to hold back his productivity and blame himself for his incompetency. As a result, the child does not develop a sense of personal worth. He eventually resents himself because he believes he is a nothing.

This self-devaluation can lead a boy or girl to delinquency. Although Ed came from a nice family and was an average student in school, he began to get the reputation as a trouble-maker by the time he was a junior in high school. Ed's parents were overdemanding ones and it didn't take long for the youth to subconsciously reason, "I don't get any attention for doing well. Maybe I'll get attention for causing trouble."

Ed realized that in today's society people get attention for extremes. He knew that basically two groups of students attracted all the attention in school: the superachievers and honor students, and the ones who were the delinquents. Ed fell in the middle in grades and aptitudes and he was simply tired of being average. He knew it would be extremely difficult to be outstandingly bright, so he decided to be extraordinary in a negative way. Ed ended up in a reformatory by the middle of his senior year..

Not all youngsters follow Ed's reasoning. Take the case of Carl, who told me, "My father expected me to do well but never rewarded my efforts. He wouldn't let me use the car nor did he give me extra money when I tried to do better. He ignored me."

By his adult years Carl had developed a "I can't win any-way" attitude. He was unwilling to extend himself in his job. In effect, Carl was saying to his boss, "I won't gain your approval no matter what I do, so why should I knock myself out?" Because his efforts and successes had gone unrewarded as a youth, Carl assumed that he would get similar reactions on the job as an adult.

Here is another example of the harm created by over-demanding parents. Judy learned at an early age that she couldn't please her mother no matter what she did. If she wore a new dress to school, Mother would tell her it was inappropriate. If Judy dusted the house, Mother would be close behind redusting or running her finger over a table top. As an adult, Judy won't make decisions or initiate action. She is afraid of being wrong. Unfortunately, she doesn't understand that not all criticism is valid and sometimes it reflects the other person's "hang ups" or personal tastes.

The Inconsistent Parents

The inconsistent home is characterized by parents who will disapprove of a youngster's action one time, but the next time it occurs will either say nothing about it or give the impression that it is cute. Such inconsistency is confusing to children because they do not learn the difference between appropriate and inappropriate behavior. Such children tend to be erratic students in school, making "A's" in one course and flunking another, often because they rarely know what their parents expect from them.

Some women are raised in an inconsistent family atmosphere where Papa is aggressive and always right and Mama is passive. Though Papa may encourage daughter to be smart and make good grades in school, he does so with the assumption that her intellect is not and should not be equal to his or any man's. A girl from this type of background often has a weak self-concept. Usually her identity is whatever her parents say she is. The girl may be brilliant, but her parents have instilled her with a notion that women are supposed to be passive and that the true meaning of life is symbolized by a wedding ring. Consequently, despite superior intelligence, such a girl will play down her mental abilities in college so she can achieve her real goal in life—marriage. Incidentally, these are the women who are now rallying to women's liberation. More on this later.

Indifferent Parents

The fourth kind of family background is the indifferent one.

These parents just aren't interested. There are no rewards, no punishments, nothing. The child can't get their attention on any count. Consequently he doesn't really know what's right and what's wrong or what yields rewards and what doesn't yield rewards.

Summary

The factors that influence your self-concept are you, your home, your friends, and other environmental elements.

However ineffective or wrong one's parents might have been, the mature person does not hang his future on his past. Nor does he allow his friends or present environment to "lead him down the garden path."

You alone must shape your own destiny. Your outlook must be: I do the best job I know how because *I* feel better for it. If *I* do a good job *I* will be rewarded and if my work is poor *I* will suffer the consequences and learn from my mistakes. I only hurt *myself,* not my parents, friends, boss or anyone else when I do not give my best to a responsibility I undertake.

Only by pushing away your emotional limits and psychological restrictions will it be possible to change your self-image from negative to positive. To do so requires a willingness to look at yourself honestly, to understand how your attitudes are revealed in actions, and to take the steps nec- to overcome self-defeating behaviors and attitudes. You will begin to like yourself by doing things which prove your self-worth.

CHAPTER III

HOW YOUR SELF-CONCEPT INFLUENCES YOUR BEHAVIOR

Need to Be Perfect

"If I'm going to be anything at all, I want the distinction of being the best. And if I can't be the best, it doesn't pay to be anything." This all or nothing attitude is not only immature, but it results in avoidance behavior.

As a draftsman Vincent was earning a below average salary. But he did not look for another job. Vincent reasoned, "Why waste my time looking for another drafting position. I'm qualified to be an engineer but no one's hiring engineers now." Notice, with this reasoning, Vincent avoids taking action, and rationalizes staying in his rut.

In Vincent's aspirations of wanting to be an engineer immediately, he was trying to shoot for the top. There is nothing wrong with this; it's what achievers do. However, if they don't make it, achievers adjust their objectives to a level they can reach. They try other routes and approaches to get what they want. Vincent, however, refused to seek a more challenging job at a higher salary, even though a new job could be a stepping stone for him. While in his rut he put forth little or no effort toward achieving his goals. His unrealistic standards became excuses for nonaction.

Once you are willing to accept the fact that you are not competing for a world title, that it's not necessary to write a Pulitzer Prize novel for you to enjoy writing, you will be able to relax and enjoy your work. This change in attitude often means that your productivity actually increases because you realize that some reward is better than none and that it's better to work diligently and regularly rather than use an "all or nothing" approach.

The need to be perfect has the tendency to slow you down with the result that you become so involved in details that you do not see the total picture. Linda who has to write reports frequently tells of this experience. She will write the first sentence of her case worker's report on a welfare family. If it doesn't sound right (and it usually doesn't), Linda keeps rewriting it until she is satisfied with it. Then she goes on to the next sentence—rewriting it several more times.

No wonder Linda doesn't get much done. She is so concerned with developing a perfect first draft that she becomes exhausted just getting the words down. Linda puts her effort into the words rather than the ideas she wants to present. Content seems to be less important than style. Because Linda is detail minded about points that matter little, she overlooks or broadly glosses over things that are important.

Linda's overconcern for how something is written, rather than what is written, almost invariably creates time pressures for her. So she has to rush through most of her reports. The result is that the first part sounds good but the rest of the report is poorly written. When Linda presents her work to her supervisor it is with the excuse that it's her first draft. Or she says she didn't have enough time to be as thorough as she would have liked.

Focusing on details is a convenient but unproductive way of not thinking about the whole. It is much easier to write a meaningful sentence than a total report, particularly if you haven't thought through all the ideas you want to present.

This difficulty can be overcome. The next time you have to write a report, try this method. Write down, without concern for wording, order or sentence structure, all the ideas you want to present. Then organize these ideas into a logical order. Once you've done this you are ready to write.

The principle is valid for nonwritten projects as well. If you can identify your overall objectives and decide on the approach you wish to take to reach them, the details will not present a major problem. More important, you will know what your end result is because you won't be relying on a piecemeal approach.

The Superman Complex

Underachievers feel that they can or should achieve success overnight or with minimum effort. In fact, this attitude is so deeply instilled that they are surprised when they hear how long it takes successful people to establish themselves. "You mean he actually struggled?", they ask of such individuals.

Their assumption that success has to be instant prevents them from taking time to learn what is required in order to do their jobs better. Learning requires time and effort. When you are learning you may even feel that you are standing still or moving backwards. This feeling can be discouraging unless you recognize that taking several steps back can be a preparation for moving forward.

Alan has been with five companies in 7 years, but he has made no progress. I asked Alan, "Why are you job hopping?"

He responded, "I wasn't getting anywhere in any of the jobs I had. So I took my experience from one job to the next."

"Has your job hopping paid off?", I asked.

"It depends how you look at it. I got a lot of experience, but no more money or responsibilities."

Alan isn't being very realistic. He naturally assumes with each job that his "brilliance" deserves immediate recognition. When this doesn't happen he is dissolutioned and seeks opportunities elsewhere. It's a kind of magical thinking process that goes on here—he thinks he is a "90 day wonder". Naturally this is a childlike viewpoint. Yet, Alan is extremely bright, one of the brightest people I've run into. But he isn't willing to exercise patience and perseverance. A person with a "superman complex" denies that he has any normal short-comings. In trying to project a superior self-image, he will assume more work than he can possibly handle. And, through "wishful thinking" believes it will get done overnight.

For these reasons it is not uncommon for such people to be involved in a variety of activities, all on a superficial level. Wanting to do everything yesterday, they wind up doing nothing today.

It is far more satisfying to pursue fewer activities, becoming proficient at them, than to tackle many with no feelings of accomplishment. It's extremely frustrating to be half good or not to complete projects you begin. Superman is a fictitious character. And, if you think you can do everything and be successful at anything with no effort, you are living in a world of make-believe.

You will find it far more rewarding to recognize your shortcomings and limitations and work through them, rather than deny their existence. Denying your shortcomings means you are ignoring reality, which may be all right for immature children, but not for adults.

Fear of Failure

No one likes to fail or be criticized for his poor performance. Since underachievers like to feel they are capable of succeeding at anything they undertake, they do not want to take the chance of destroying this unrealistic notion. Consequently, they would rather maintain the excuse that they are lazy than to actually try, and possibly risk failure. After all, if their total effort did not produce results, what excuse could they use? By avoiding efforts to achieve and by taking elaborate precautions to prevent being labeled a failure, they also avoid success. Their actions reflect the old proverb "nothing ventured, nothing gained."

The fear of failure, rather than being admitted and overcome, has a paralytic effect. It is revealed in self-defeating actions which will fulfill their prophecy that they will fail. In other words, one fails because he fears failure and he does virtually nothing to prove that there was no real basis for the fear.

A freelance writer I know who is terrified of failing makes it a point to write articles and stories that he feels are sure sellers. He avoids controversial topics and sticks to interviewing people he knows are receptive to him. Bob's excuse is that "I won't get a good interview from someone who is antagonistic to the press, and, if he's involved in a controversial field, he won't want to talk to me anyway."

If Bob is pressured by an editor to do an interview with a person who is not known for his cooperation with journalists, Bob will spend a great deal of time getting in the mood and preparing himself for the interview. When he is psychologically ready Bob makes a halfhearted attempt at asking leading questions. Since he's already convinced that he won't get a good interview he is less than creative in his approach. He is also unenthusiastic and bores the subject with trite, ordinary questions. So Bob is given ordinary answers and hustled out as soon as possible.

Now Bob can safely report to his editor, "I told you so." The rejection is not even particularly painful to Bob because he fully expected it.

People, like Bob, use similar avoidance reasoning when faced with competition or other high risk (to their egos) activities. They prefer to avoid competition rather than take the chance of losing.

One's fear of failure can also be reflected when writing reports. Those who have business positions will rarely submit to their superiors a finished version of a report. It is usually a draft. This tactic serves two functions. First, if the report is criticized, it's not a major catastrophe because it was submitted under the guise of a rough draft. Second, he does not have to assume the responsibility of putting forth his best effort. It is much easier to pull together a rough draft than to prepare a finished product. Furthermore, because he is afraid that even his best attempts will not be well received, he protects himself by handing in sloppy work. In doing so he guards his untested and unrealistic self-image of "I could do a good job if I really tried."

Using these tactics to avoid the possibility of failure results in an image of amateurism. The individual simply gives the appearance of being a superficial worker who lacks pride in his work. Achievers, on the other hand, are willing to take the risk of failure. But these are calculated risks based on self-disciplined action and a desire to be judged on the basis of their best efforts. An achiever will write a report, read it, make corrections and then put it aside, reworking it later if necessary. Then, when he is happy with the report, he submits it to his superior, ready to receive whatever criticism it deserves. The achiever views criticism as a learning experience, not as a personal attack.

Many housewives who say they would like to return to the job market have a similiar fear of failure. I've counseled women who want to go back to work and who are continuously griping about housework. In such cases I'll ask them, "Why don't you get yourself a part time job?"

"My husband wouldn't want me to," the housewife usually replies.

"Have you talked to him about it?" I ask.

The typical response here is, "Not really." When I probe further, saying, "Why haven't you asked your husband?" most housewives in this situation will say, "Chances are he wouldn't let me."

What is happening here is that the housewife is making negative assumptions rather than risk failure. She is really afraid to apply for a part time job because she might not be as successful in the business world as she is in her homemaking. Yet she is frustrated because she doesn't feel that being a housewife is as challenging as it once was. So she puts all the blame for her frustrations on her husband and makes excuses instead of trying to overcome her misery. After all, she will no longer have an excuse to be miserable if she gets a part time job and fails at it.

Fear of Success

Success and achievement carry responsibilities. Others

expect you to maintain the pace and standards you have established. In addition, you are judged according to these standards. The pressure to perform consistently at a high level is more than many underachievers want to cope with.

A computer salesman I knew was earning $12,000 in a territory that should have been yielding him substantially more. His wife was fairly content with his income, but his boss was not. When we discussed the situation Harry related his dilemma. "If I earned more money," he said, "my wife would spend more and she would expect me to maintain my new income. This would mean that I would be under great pressure; I'm not sure I want it. Frankly, I don't know if I'm capable of earning more on a consistent basis. This way I'm at a level I know I can keep up with."

When I asked Harry if he was content with his performance, he replied, "No, I'm not. But I might be worse off the other way."

We see in this situation a dual problem. On the one hand, Harry is afraid that success will force him to work harder just to maintain it. At the same time, he is afraid he doesn't have what it takes to be successful. These concerns, or fears, also caused Harry to be unhappy with himself because he wasn't utilizing his potential.

I recommended that he throw himself into his job. Harry reluctantly agreed. A year later he was earning more than double his original income. More important, he felt a sense of personal satisfaction because he was making the most of his capabilities. True, Harry felt the pressures of fulfilling the new goals he had established for himself. But he was also pleased at his new found energy and sense of accomplishment.

Another example of the consequences from the fear of success is seen in Sharon's behavior. An excellent writer, Sharon had developed her history Ph.D. thesis into a book. But she still hasn't submitted it to a publisher and it's been months since it was completed. Sharon's fiance can't understand why she doesn't do anything with the manuscript.

This way Sharon can tell about how the book is going to be a best seller and how successful it will be in academic circles without putting it to the test. She can dream about the end results without carrying through. Granted, Sharon has achieved a certain accomplishment in putting together a book. She has gone half way, but she is afraid of going all the way because it means that someone else will have to pass judgment. Sharon enjoys hearing her fiance rave about how good the book is and she likes all the compliments she gets from friends and acquaintances. But, she is terrified of the personal pressures that a successfully completed book would create.

If fear of success is a problem, the main questions you have to ask are these: Am I better off emotionally just getting by than I would be if I committed myself wholly to my job? If I succeeded, what benefits would I gain and what are the possible consequences? If I enjoy my work, wouldn't it be more gratifying financially and personally to extend myself and do more of it? Your responses to each of these questions should provide you with valid reasons for wanting to achieve. The rewards you will gain from success generally outweigh the validity of your anticipated fears.

Even if your total efforts do not produce the results you expect, you will be doing somewhat better than you have in the past. Isn't this slight reward worth the extra energy you must put forth?

Other Negative Self-Concept Actions

Many assume that if they are self-deprecating and contrite with people they will gain special consideration and that these actions will draw attention away from what is actually expected of them. They believe that if they let others know how bad they feel about their poor performance they will be excused.

So, they approach others with an embarrassed, highly apologetic, "please forgive me" attitude, as if the whole world has come to an end. They demean themselves and give the the impression that they want the persons whom they have disappointed to berate them. They feel that by being reprimanded it will excuse their failure to deliver.

The fact is that such action is inappropriate. All it does is reinforce the negative image others already have of you. It also makes people feel uncomfortable. When you can't finish a project say so without further deprecating yourself. You are not helping yourself when you are being self-destructive.

Boyish bravado is another method used by many to escape from getting things done. They seem to have the notion that if they make a joke out of everything people will like them better and not expect as much from them. Consequently, they give the impression that life, and work in particular, do not have great meaning to them. They really don't want to be taken seriously because that would mean that they have to produce. More often than not, they succeed in conveying this clownish impression. So they are rarely given challenges or work which is truly important.

Many will exaggerate the importance of small successes, focusing on them as if they are saying, "See what I've accomplished. What else do you expect from me?" They tend to use these minor successes as excuses for loafing and sitting on their potential. Once they feel they are "off the hook," they continue to be as nonproductive as always. These successes appease the ego and remove some of the pressure to achieve.

In some cases this tendency to magnify minor successes serves to hold back someone who has the ability to be a successful achiever. An insurance salesman I know has the nasty habit of doing nothing, other than bragging about his results, whenever he's ahead. As a consequence of Gary's do-nothing behavior, he falls behind after a couple of weeks. Gary is almost always under pressure because he gloats about his accomplishments rather than forging ahead to maintain the pace. Thus, he must work twice as hard to catch up.

Gary exaggerates small successes because it is important for him to endorse himself and to convince others of his value. Unfortunately, he spends more time talking about his worth than demonstrating it. Achievers, however, take successes in stride. They prefer to move on to the next challenge with little fanfare.

These self-depreciating actions do nothing more than establish an image which is difficult to live down—that of an overgrown adolescent. And, unless you make a conscious effort to change, you will not be able to get out of this self-created trap.

To change this image it is necessary to be honest with yourself. If you do not like, approve of, or are not able to do what you are supposed to do, make it known to those who can help you. Let them know of your sincere feeling and concerns. The devious routes of contriteness, boyish bravado and bragging accomplish nothing.

CHAPTER IV

YOUR RELATIONS WITH OTHERS

Why Doesn't Everybody Love Me?

Most mature people choose their friends discriminately. They know they can't appeal to or please everyone, just as not everyone pleases them. So they don't even try. They develop relationships with those friends and acquaintances who have meaning to them and they disregard those people they don't care for.

Must you be loved by everyone? Does anyone and everyone you meet *have* to like you? If they don't, do you feel slighted and hurt? Chances are, this need to be liked is so strong that it is often carried to extremes. For example, even people you meet casually for the first time are viewed in terms of: "I wonder if I made a good impression?" Your concern over the impression you make on people who don't really mean anything to you occupies much of your thinking time.

But why? Aren't there people *you* dislike? If you have the right and good sense to dislike some people, why can't others be disinterested in you? What makes you so special that you can be discriminating but others can't? Can you honestly be all things to all people? Obviously you can't unless you are so plastic that you can change your personality at a moment's notice. And, even if you are a plastic person, some people still won't like you. So why sacrifice your values and principles (which is what you must do if you want to please everyone) for a goal you know can't be achieved?

While you're thinking about these questions, let's explore how your need to be accepted and liked by everyone gets you in trouble. Because a good deal of your energy is directed toward pleasing others, you will not turn down a request regardless of how unreasonable it may be. You will, when asked, volunteer for anything. You promise to have assignments and projects ready even though you know you can't deliver. In your effort to please, you generally assume greater responsibilities than can possibly be accomplished because you invariably underestimate the amount of time it takes to do a project.

Admittedly, some of these behaviors are a result of your failure to plan ahead. But your difficulty in saying "no" to people, and your assumption that if you agree to requests others will like you more for it, are contributing factors. You really want the other person to gush, "Oh, you're so wonderful and so great to do this for me."

While these appear to be "nice guy" gestures, they turn against you because you usually do *not* deliver the goods. Because you set unrealistic time limits on yourself, it is probably common for you to be late in turning in assignments and in keeping appointments. Many who overcommit themselves have to back out of their promises. Or, they conveniently forget about them.

Ironically, because you fail to come through with your commitments you create the very impression you want to avoid. Others view your actions as irresponsible and immature. You inadvertently develop a reputation of "talking a better game than you play." No one likes, believes or trusts a person who makes commitments and promises he can't fulfill, or whose words are not backed up by action. Nor do others care for people who can only be counted on to make excuses.

Let me assure you that most people would prefer forthrightness and sincerity even though it might result in revised plans. Others are also capable of accepting a refusal in good faith. They would prefer that you do not accept a request or volunteer for some service if you cannot devote the time. They would also rather that you accurately estimate (or even overestimate) a completion date on a project instead of promising an early delivery date that does not materialize.

In their desire to please, underachievers make these useless promises because they have projected their own attitudes onto someone else. Suppose Polly is asked, "When will you have this report done?" Her typical reasoning and response goes like this: "Chances are that my boss wants me to have this report done tomorrow. So I will say tomorrow. It doesn't matter what I think; I want to please him."

What happens when tomorrow comes and Polly doesn't have the report done? She says, "Gee, I didn't realize the report would take this long. When do you want it?" Though Polly forces her superior to give a time, she will again underestimate and promise the report a day or so earlier than he said. The circle continues and Polly is constantly making excuses.

Why did Polly act this way in the first place? She sincerely wanted to please her boss and she assumed that this was what he wanted. Such action is unproductive—Polly is being dishonest with herself as well as with her boss. Because she is always trying to please everybody she ends up pleasing no one. Achievers, however, have a certain integrity. They aren't going to make any promises they can't keep.

Everyone should remember that people don't like you any less for being sincere and honest with them. If you can't do something, let it be known. You *can* be liked and respected without sacrificing your self-esteem, basic values and integrity.

Those I have counseled have been pleasantly surprised when they take my advice to refuse requests they cannot fulfill and to avoid making promises they cannot keep. They discover that what I tell them is true: others respect them for leveling. More important, a person gains greater respect for *himself* when he accepts tasks he can do and turns his back on those he can't. Such behavior creates the impression that your actions speak as loud as your words.

Another symptom of the compelling need to please others was revealed to me by an engineer. Hank said, "Even when I have good intentions of following a plan of action, it goes awry because of interruptions. I usually plan to take the first half hour in the morning to organize myself for the day. But it doesn't work that way. Just as I begin to organize my work, I am interrupted by different people or by phone calls."

"Why not tell your secretary that you do not wish to be disturbed until you are ready to receive calls or people?" I asked.

"Because," Hank said, "I don't want to hurt their feelings. I just can't say no."

This man was so concerned about what others thought of him that he hurt himself the most in his attempts to please others. Because he could not bring himself to be straightforward and honest with people he paid a steep penalty. Hank did not get his work done and had to work after hours as well as weekends to catch up. *He* was the one who was always running behind and therefore he got left behind. As expected, Hank resented those who cut in on his time and "forced" him to be self-sacrificial. Because his resentment showed through, he created less than adequate relationships with others. Hank's attempt to be well liked exploded in his face.

Many people unintentionally harm others in their efforts to be "nice guys." A manager I knew had difficulties developing the sales abilities of his subordinates. Unless they were good salemen to begin with, Russell could not deal effectively with them. He was unsuccessful in bringing out the best from potentially good employees who, in his estimation, were performing below par.

When I asked Russell what he said to those subordinates who were not producing according to his expectations, he said, "I don't say anything."

"Why not?" I asked.

"Because I don't want to offend them. My men like me; I wouldn't do anything to destroy that feeling."

"How do you get them to improve?"

"I don't. I just let them hang themselves. They eventually realize that they are not cut out for this work and they quit."

Here is a man who literally killed people with kindness. If Russell wasn't trying so hard to be liked he would realize that his attitudes are selfish. Because he was overly sensitive about what others thought of him, he avoided the risk of an argument or disagreement. Russell was not being helpful to his subordinates when he failed to confront them honestly and directly with their shortcomings. As a result, both lost. The manager lost potentially productive employees, who could have been outstanding with some direction, and the employees lost because they did not receive the benefit of this manager's counsel.

A more fruitful technique for dealing with this problem would be to tell a subordinate that you are dissatisfied with his performance. Then work out with him a course of action that will help him improve. This approach is appreciated because it clearly shows that you have interest in him as an employee and as a person. Yes, the initial criticism may sting momentarily. But such feelings are easily overshadowed by your willingness to help subordinates overcome their difficulties. All you have to do is remember that criticism need not be offensive. If directed toward a person's actions it can be helpful and be received enthusiastically.

Of course, problems arise when a person feels that he as an individual is being criticized. Let's say that a fellow employee did not provide some information you needed to complete your work. If you were to say to him, "You are undependable," he would rightfully interpret the comment as a slap in the face. After all, it's not likely that he is undependable in every respect. This kind of comment attacks his total being.

But would you get the same response if you said, "I need such and such information and I'm disappointed that you don't have it ready. When can I have it?" Here, you are criticizing a particular instance of undependability rather than the total person. It's one thing to disapprove of an action—a different matter to disapprove of a person.

You can learn to criticize without being caustic and giving a verbal acid bath. One way is to offer alternatives to the person you are criticizing. Instead of saying, "You did a lousy job," say, "I would prefer it if you would have done it this way." Another approach is to indicate that your expectations have not been fulfilled and you are disappointed. In this way you are allowing the other party to be self-critical or to apologize if he wants to.

Some "nice guys" have such a desire to be helpful that they interfere in others' affairs. Hoping that amicable assistance will bring them love, these individuals will give unrequested advice and do things for others without first receiving their consent. This may be your problem if people accuse you of meddling in their affairs. More often than not, people resent this immature way of giving help. Most individuals don't like to have you run their life for them.

An indiscriminate desire to help others (an "I want to be of service to my fellow man, even if it kills him" attitude) is really very self-centered. The reasoning here is: "*I* feel better for it and *I* will be liked for it, so why not?" There's no thought of whether the other person will feel better or whether your actions will truly aid him.

Achievers are less motivated by a desire to be liked. Those who are sincerely interested in helping others are more interested in the other person than in their selfish interests. An achiever will not impose his help. Rather, he will offer to help, giving others the option of rejecting or accepting the offer.

In short, you can be better liked if you do not try so hard. If you don't make your desire to be well-liked obvious, you will make more friends and acquaintances.

The Pain of Aloneness

Most underachievers need to be around people constantly. But they do not relate to others on a mature, give-and-take level. Instead, they unwittingly place themselves in a subservient and demeaning position. They continually ask advice, seek approval and let others know how much they are needed. Such action places you in a vulnerable position because others recognize your weaknesses and take advantage of them.

This inability to tolerate being alone serves as an excuse for lack of productive activity. "How can I ignore people?" They ask themselves. Since they can't, they consider it perfectly legitimate to postpone work that has to be done now in order to socialize. It is more fun and less taxing to socialize than to concentrate on a task that requires self-discipline.

In short, he seeks out people and then blames them or uses them as an excuse for not getting his work done. Even when others initiate the contact, the inability to say, "I'm sorry, but I'm busy now" also stems from his need to please and not offend others.

To avoid this self-defeating pitfall, become involved only in what you have to do. Try to shut out all distractions because what you are doing is important to you. Let the project you are working on take the place of socialization. You must learn to be comfortable with yourself and your work. Remember: if you are not interesting to yourself and do not enjoy your own company, others are likely to feel the same way. If you learn to like yourself, others will like you too. If you become secure with yourself, mature relationships will follow.

The "Should" Complex

Underachievers pay a handsome price for being "nice guys" and for sacrificing themselves to please others. Many dislike themselves for making commitments they can't deliver, for not saying to others what is bothering them, and for socializing when they ought to be working. Their assumption that they will lose favor with people if they are forthright and assertive forces them to do things that are distasteful and possibly damaging to their career and personal goals. It is common for underachievers to make erroneous assumptions about other people's expectations of them. Instead of asking a spouse or a boss what is expected, they spend considerable time talking to themselves. This is a typical monologue: "I *should* accept his request. If I don't he'll think less of me. He might even be disappointed in me if I refuse him. Sure, I'll tell him that I'll do it. That will get him off my back for a while anyway."

Actions that stem from these "should" and "if I don't—then" types of monologues are self-defeating and result in unnecessary emotional turmoil. You are constantly struggling to simultaneously satisfy two demands—those you should do and those you want to do. Often, these demands do not coincide.

Walter, who was trained in social work, left his field for a career in market research because he thought his wife wanted him to earn more money. He gave up social work for a business career simply because he believed that he should do it to please his wife. His own interests and desires were subjugated by a "should" complex.

Three years later, Walter *was* earning more money in market research. But he was miserable. When he came to me to discuss his problem, he had already changed jobs three times and was contemplating another move. Aside from being unhappy with this type of work, Walter was having headaches and complained of stomach pains.

When I advised him to tell his wife that he could no longer sacrifice his life just to please her, he balked, but eventually took my suggestion. Much to Walter's surprise, his wife was not interested in more money if it required him to do work he did not like. Once he realized his assumptions were false, he reentered the field he had given up and is now progressing at a rapid rate.

The "should" complex serves an important, but not very productive function. It allows you to set up a "straw man" who gives you an excuse for nonachievement. You can blame others for your failure to assume responsibility for your actions or nonactions. If you do something because you should, rather than because you want to, you can excuse your failure by saying, "I didn't want to do it anyway. It's not my fault that it didn't turn out." You always have a scapegoat.

The former social worker I referred to rationalized his lack of success in market research by saying, "It's not the field I really wanted; I'm doing it for my wife." Students who do poorly in school say, "My parents want me to go to college. They think it's the thing to do. I could care less about being a scholar." Housewives who have sloppy homes with unwashed dishes, unmade beds and dust thick enough to write on, rationalize, "I wanted to be a lawyer. My creativity and ability is stifled. Why did my husband ask me to get married when he did?" These excuses demonstrate a key characteristic of underachievers: they do not want to take responsibility for their decisions.

Admittedly, there are certain things you *should* do. But unless such behavior is balanced against your values and principles, it can be personally damaging. In short, you *should* be truthful to yourself. Your actions should lead toward self-fulfillment. If you can't look at yourself in the mirror and be satisfied with the image you present, what good are you to others?

Another consequence of the "should" complex appears after a confrontation with another person. Although an individual avoids arguments, he also castigates himself for several days following a confrontation. He mulls over all the things he should have said or done in that situation. He broods about these "shoulds" for days and sometimes weeks.

What he does not realize is that his unwillingness to say what is really on his mind interferes with his physical and mental well-being. Failure to express your anger puts stress on your body—and stress can lead to ulcers, high blood pressure and severe headaches.

The whole person, the person who is at peace with himself, generally has calm, healthy bodily functions. This is the individual whose actions and words are fairly close; one reflects the other. But if a person feels one thing and acts in a completely different way, something has got to give in the system. If you feel angry enough to yell at a person but are nice instead, what does this do to you inside? Although they don't realize it, people describe what literally happens to the body's chemistry when they say, "I churn inside" or "I boil." This boiling has an effect on certain organs in your body— you get ulcers, you boil yourself into a high blood pressure situation or into a heart condition.

Being afraid to say what he really thinks because he worries about the opinions of others, the underachiever is often angry. He just doesn't show it in a very obvious way. Dennis, for example, was a heavy drinker who began to complain about stomach pains. Whenever he felt angry at his boss, his job or his wife, he wouldn't express it. He would go to a nearby tavern and drink.

I asked Dennis, "Why are you drinking? Why don't you say how you feel to your wife?"

"I don't want to make her angry. I don't want to upset her. I'm afraid that if I really get angry, I'll blow up and I'll regret it."

"So what do you do? You go and get drunk. You take it out on yourself," I told him.

There are a number of people in mental institutions who do this very same thing. They continually hurt themselves physically and emotionally. They make all kinds of assumptions about what another person is going to do or not going to do. And they answer themselves. The world is all in them; there's no sharing it with anyone else. Something in the system will break down.

From an emotional standpoint, it is healthier to vent your feelings than to hold them in. This is why we get relief from talking to professionals or friends about problems that bother us. I am not saying that you have to constantly argue. But you are not being fair to others or to yourself when your actions do not reflect your true feelings.

I always ask my patients, "Why don't you say what you

mean and do what you feel?" The typical response is a mumbled, "Because of people." So I ask them two more questions: "What is the worst thing that can happen? How bad is that?" In most instances, the thing that can happen is nowhere near as bad as what's happening to them emotionally and physically right then.

What usually happens is that you store up your angry feelings until a minor incident occurs that makes you react completely out of proportion to the event. Suppose you are dissatisfied with certain aspects of your job. If you are an underachiever you would complain vigorously to co-workers and friends but never to your boss, even though he could probably resolve your problem constructively. Rather than talk to your boss about your concerns, your tendency is to *wish* he would sense your dissatisfactions. When he doesn't, you keep building your case against the job. Finally, even a question asking you to clarify a point in a report may cause you to quit. Or, you become nonproductive and get fired.

You could prevent such consequences by expressing your feelings to your superior so that you get feedback from him. You would know where you stand. Isn't this a more mature way of handling a situation? True, the reaction you get may be unpleasant. But isn't that feeling less painful than wondering where you stand? In the long run, being yourself will be more personally and professionally satisfying than trying to be a chameleon.

The "should" complex is so deeply ingrained into underachievers that they generalize and apply it to others. They have inordinately high expectations of people and believe that others *should* be perfect and flawless. They set up false gods who invariably have the clay feet of humans. Because no one can meet such impossible and unrealistic standards, underachievers are constantly disappointed in others.

Their disappointments are reflected in a tendency to be hypercritical of people. By focusing on the weaknesses of others, these individuals are able to justify their own failings. Their line of reasoning goes like this: "If others are not pulling their weight, why should I?" Or, "The boss is not working as hard as he should, so why should I?"

Many college students typically use the instructors as scapegoats for their own inadequate performance. Ellen, a music major in college, had a B average until she started taking some of the required courses outside her major field. Then her grades plummeted to C's and D's. Ellen was used to small classes and individual attention from her professors, which she got in abundance at the music school. But the introductory American government political science course had 250 students attending lectures three days a week. The lecturer was not even a professor—which bothered Ellen. And he seldom gave his students an opportunity to ask questions about the material in class.

Not wanting to seek out the lecturer during his office hours or ask some of her classmates for help, Ellen plodded along. She took excellent, almost voluminous notes in her music classes, but rarely jotted down more than a sentence or two in political science. Not surprisingly, Ellen flunked the midterm examination. She wasn't too upset because she didn't believe that it was really her fault.

"The professor isn't teaching like he should. Why should I study if he doesn't know how to teach?" Ellen asked. She eked through with a D for the course simply because she didn't want to take it over again. Only that thought could provide her with *some* incentive to study. But she wasn't *really* going to study because of the stupid lecturer who had no rapport with his students, according to Ellen.

These criticisms, while they may be valid, do nothing to help you achieve. So what if someone else is not doing his work. Is that a valid reason for you not to do yours? After all, your performance is not judged by what others do or don't do. For example, if Ellen does not study because the instructor is poor, who pays the consequences? Similarly, if a worker doesn't do his best because others are not carrying their load, he fails (as do the others) to develop in his job.

Achievers, in contrast, reason differently. They know that

no one is perfect. Hence, achievers rarely are disappointed when people don't fulfill their promises or when they neglect their duties. Achievers really don't care what others should be or are not doing. They have learned to rely on their own resources and look to others for support only when necessary. Because achievers have a mature outlook toward people, they benefit from their strengths and are less affected by their weaknesses.

This attitude allows achievers to be more aware of themselves and their activities. They complete their objectives because they have a "how can I do" rather than a "why not to do" philosophy.

The "What If" Complex

Self-defeating behavior results from other false and unconfirmed assumptions. These I call the "what if" complex because nonaction or nonproductive reactions are based upon unsubstantiated beliefs that certain behaviors will result in disaster. For example, underachievers will not ask for a raise even if it is appropriate because, "What if he won't give it to me?" Or, they won't look for another job because, "What if I don't find one. and my boss hears that I'm looking?" Or, they won't approach their boss with a problem because, "What if he doesn't have time to discuss it with me?"

People who exhibit the "what if" complex anticipate that their actions will be met with resistance, if not completely rebuked. Since it is potentially dangerous (their egos may be bruised) to take an aggressive stand with others, these individuals prefer to be passive.

Frequently the "what if" complex is expressed as an assertive statement of probability. "He probably will turn down my request" or "He probably will get angry at me if I tell him that I can't do it."

If asked, "How do you know?" The usual answer is "I just know; I feel it." Behind these unsubstantiated assertions and anticipated fears is the concern that they will be rejected.

If you don't ask there's no danger of being turned down; you are insulated from this fate when you do not initiate action. Of course, by not taking such risks you limit your progress.

Dealing With These Complexes

Unfortunately, many of your assumptions are wrong more often than right. Jess wanted to take a week off from work to handle some personal business. He was struggling with the question of whether he should or should not ask his supervisor. Jess was going through the usual "what if," "if I do— then" and "he'll probably" types of mental exercises.

I finally asked him, "What's the worst thing that can happen to you if you make the request?"

Jess said, "The worst thing that can happen is that he'd say 'no'."

"How bad is that?" I replied. "Does his refusal of your request diminish your worth as a man?"

Jess thought for a moment and said, "No, of course not. But it would make me feel bad."

"How bad do you feel not knowing what he would say?"

"That makes me feel bad too; it keeps me wondering."

"Well, then, you've got little to lose and a great deal to gain by asking."

Convinced of my final statement, Jess made his request and was surprised when it was granted. He realized, at least for the moment, that a refusal does not mean you're being rejected as a person. If a request is denied or someone's opinion differs from yours, remember that your opinions and points of view are as reasonable as the next person's.

Sometimes your inability to take action because of false assumptions will cause you to act as Larry did. He was unhappy in his job. He had another position to go to, but he really didn't want to leave the company he'd worked for since college graduation.

I asked Larry, "Could the company have done anything about your job?"

"Yes, there are other things I could have done with my training."

"Why don't you talk to your boss about it?"

"I might get fired," Larry said.

"You're planning to quit anyway. What's the worst thing that can happen to you?" I asked.

"The worst thing is that I get fired."

"What's the best thing that can happen?"

"The situation will be changed."

"Now, suppose you don't tell the boss about your problem. The worst thing that can happen is that you leave the job one way or the other. So you can't lose by asking," I pointed out.

As it turned out, Larry did ask and the company gave him another job that he liked much better.

Much unproductive mental and emotional energy can be conserved, unnecessary second guessing can be avoided, and the self-defeating nature of these "should" and "what if" complexes can be reduced. When faced with a confrontation or other face-to-face interpersonal problem, ask yourself these questions:

1. Are my assumptions correct? If you are not sure, ask yourself:

2. What's the worst thing that can happen by saying what is on my mind? How bad is that?

3. If I am rebuked on an issue that is vitally important to me, do I want to continue dealing with that person?

4. When another person rejects my request or idea, is it a personal reflection on me or is he simply expressing one viewpoint? Is his viewpoint necessarily more right than mine even if it differs from mine?

5. Why should I? And if I do what I "should,"
am I sacrificing my personal values?

By asking yourself these questions you put the other person in a realistic perspective. Even experts on the same subject disagree. This does not make them any less worthy of being called "expert."

I am not suggesting that it is unwise to anticipate or to make certain assumptions about other's intentions. Analyzing a situation has value in that it provides you with a basis for making sounder decisions. The problem arises when avoidance of action, excuses for nonproductive action and wheel-spinning occur as a result of over analysis or unfounded assumptions.

CHAPTER V

THE FAMISHED EGO

Please Pay Attention to Me

Everyone needs some attention—the ego is a very hungry "organism". Recognition provides you with tangible evidence that you are important, not just a body or a number and that your efforts are worthwhile. Achievers gain attention through their accomplishments. Others respect them for getting projects done and for working diligently toward achieving the objectives they set. Achievers themselves feel a sense of personal worth from the recognition they receive as well as the satisfaction of utilizing their potential. The achiever feeds his "famished ego" through accomplishments.

Underachievers rarely have their ego hunger satisfied because their methods for feeding it are often ineffective and inappropriate. Many erroneously assume that they are the center of attention and that others are always watching them when they are in fact not the most important person in a group. As far as they are concerned, the world revolves around them.

Such assumptions, when not valid, increase their pressure to "entertain" others, even when this action is not requested. In short, they feel they are on display when they are really not. Because of these assumptions, they will say and do things to draw attention to themselves rather than to their accomplishments.

For example, Nina talks constantly about herself in conversations with co-workers and friends. She boasts about minor and insignificant achievements: "I've been on my diet for two weeks and lost three whole pounds." Or Nina exaggerates her own importance by weaving little stories about social events. "There I was, asking the Senator what he thought about women's rights," Nina will say, when all she did was hover near the fringe area of a coffee klatch during the last election.

In listening to Nina one gets the impression that she is unaware of the world around her; elements outside of herself interest her little. Consequently Nina presents the image of a braggart with an inflated ego. In reality, she is desperately trying to prove her worth. Nina is really very insecure and lacking in confidence.

Nina sincerely wants to belong to a group. So she often settles for a listener, not necessarily a rapt one, who will let her talk about herself. But it isn't interesting to talk to Nina about Nina. So she frequently moves from group to group, usually in a peripheral relationship. What she does not realize is that few people are that interested in her. Others are too wrapped up in themselves to notice or listen to anyone else.

Like most underachievers, if Nina receives an unsolicited compliment she cannot accept it graciously. If you tell Nina, "You've done a nice job on this," she is likely to respond with such comments as: "You don't mean it, do you?" or "It wasn't as good as it could have been." These responses really mean: "I wish you'd convince me that it's as good as you say because I think so little of myself that I need your reassurance."

When such individuals fail to gain the attention they want from others, they withdraw. They pout, become despondent or become angry at those who do not give them the attention they feel they deserve. At the same time, because they are too self-centered to think about offering their help to others, they unwittingly gain the reputation of being selfish. In effect this behavior produces the very reactions they want to avoid.

If you rely *exclusively* on others to build up your ego, you are relying on undependable and unstable sources. You cannot, nor should you, count on others to perform a service that you can perform for yourself. I recommend that whenever you do something that you believe is worthy of praise, congratulate yourself. You have to approve of your own actions and like what you are doing if you are going to present a confident image to others. You have to have convictions about yourself that you *are* somebody and you *have* done something worthwhile. Self-endorsement can be a valuable and lasting source of ego building.

Naturally you do many things which deserve recognition and approval. If you look to yourself for such endorsements, you will diminish your ego hunger. After all, you can compliment yourself as often as you need. Don't degrade yourself. Why should anyone else feel differently if you can't think highly of yourself? As a way of developing this self-endorsement habit, ask yourself: "What did I do today that was worthwhile?" Then compliment yourself for it.

Other Attention Getting Tactics

When underachievers do not gain recognition through productive efforts they will turn to nonproductive means. Many spend their time wishing for things to happen. They even make it a point to tell others of their elaborate hopes and plans for achieving greatness: "Some day I will have a big house, write a book, be president of the company and be rich."

Of course these are pipe dreams with no foundations. It's as if you are saying: "If I can't gain attention for doing, maybe others will respect me for my intentions to do." Being magical thinkers, they assume that if they wish hard enough something will happen which will save them from drudgery. Maybe a fortune will come their way or perhaps they will be "discovered" by someone. These daydreams often take the place of action. Hence, they are frustrated and disillusioned with themselves because they live in a world of make-believe.

The fact is that personal satisfaction does not come from dreaming or talking about accomplishments. If you used this time to actually work on your plans and take the necessary steps to make your dream a reality, you would feel better. More often than not, those who talk about all the things they are going to do use up whatever ambitious thoughts they have in talking. After a while there is little energy remaining in activating these ideas.

What happens when your wishes do not materialize? How do you explain your lack of accomplishments to others as well as to yourself? A common defensive tactic is to complain vigorously about your problems—both physical and personal—to anyone you meet. When someone asks, "How are you?", you interpret the question literally and view it as an opportunity to vividly describe all problems.

Because underachievers are constantly looking for sympathy and therapy, anyone who shows the slightest interest in them becomes their personal psychologist. They use their problems as an excuse for nonachievement and for gaining special consideration. In effect they are saying: "Poor me. How can you expect me to accomplish anything with all the troubles I've got? Don't you see, you've got to expect less of me." They are also suggesting in an indirect way that their superiors lower their standards.

Scott, an accountant, told me that when he works late on a project he makes it a point to let everyone in the office know how hard he's been working. When I asked him why he does this, Scott said, "Because I don't want anyone to expect much from me that day. It's a way of protecting myself from being judged as lazy when I'm coasting."

Some nonproductive people have daydreams of becoming seriously ill or incapacitated. They secretly hope their daydreams will come true so that others will feel sorry for them. Suffering heroes tend to bring out the charitable characteristics in others. Or to put it more bluntly, if you can't get attention by succeeding, maybe you can get it by being helpless. Such daydreams are wishes to escape from responsibility.

These suffering hero daydreams frequently become a reality. Psychosomatic illnesses are common self-fulfilling prophecies. For example, Dick started complaining about headaches and stomach pains shortly after he was given responsibility for a new management training program. He began to dwell on his symptoms and used them as excuses for turning in his recommendations so slowly. Eventually Dick developed an ulcer and he wasn't particularly upset at the diagnosis. For Dick, the ailment's manifestation was proof: "I told you I was sick and this proves it."

It is interesting to note that achievers who become ill do not react in the same immature manner. They either cope with it with little fuss or seek medical care until cured.

Pipe dreams, suffering hero daydreams and complaining may gain attention, but not respect. Such avoidance behavior does nothing more than advance one's self-defeating behavior and enlarge his weaknesses. He becomes more and more convinced that he is incapable of achieving success because he concentrates on his negative qualities.

Although this may be a surprise to you, most people don't really care to hear your complaints. When they ask, "How are you?" it is just a social pleasantry. They don't want you to take them literally. They're not interested in your medical history. So the next time you feel like complaining about your ills and pains, whether true or imaginary, don't do it.

Aside from the fact that few people are truly interested, indiscriminate complaining is emotionally taxing and time consuming for you. When you tell others of your problems you are draining yourself of potential productive energy. You are only creating a "pity me" mental state. Therefore, if the person you are complaining to doesn't feel sorry for you, you do. I'm sure you can recall many times when you thought or talked about a depressing situation. The more you discussed it with someone else, the more intense the depression became. After a while you became so upset that you were unable to do anything.

You can avoid this semi-depressive, intellectually paralyzing condition. The next time someone asks you, "How are you?" simply say, "I'm fine." By saying this you may even feel fine. Whenever possible, avoid complaining about problems and issues you cannot change. You cannot permanently run away from responsibility by feigning illness or daydreaming it. In the final analysis such tactics do nothing for your ego or your physical well being.

CHAPTER VI

HOW ORGANIZED ARE YOU?

Why Things Don't Get Done

An achiever budgets his hours and his energies. Whether he's brushing his teeth or driving a car, he thinks of nothing except what he's doing at the moment. He doesn't let problems bother him until he is ready to deal with the problem on a total basis.

This attitude is foreign to underachievers. They cannot cope with the idea of doing one thing at a time and not letting anything else get in the way. Many drift thru life. They start off in the morning not knowing where they are going. They just go—disregarding the fact that they have no direction or destination. Typically, they have difficulties managing time, ordering priorities, overcoming inertia, and directing or focusing their efforts. They also have a tendency to magnify problems out of proportion to reality. These paralyzing obstacles explain why they are under constant stress and rarely have a sense of accomplishment.

The feeling that accompanies such stress was revealed to me by a university professor named Todd. "I have so many things to do and feel them all pressing down on me at the same time that I don't know where to begin," he said.

"What do you do to relieve this pressure?" I asked.

"Most of the time," Todd told me, "I'll start to work on something—anything that seems important at the moment.

Before I make a dent, I begin something else. Then I realize that the paper I'm working on is not as pressing as some other project that's sitting on my desk. Before I notice what has happened, two or three hours pass by with no results to show for the time I've spent."

In order to better understand Todd's problem, I visited his office. His desk was piled with a variety of papers, books and pamphlets. He was sitting in front of his desk, shuffling one paper here, a book there.

"What are you doing?" I asked.

"To tell you the truth, I was just trying to decide what I ought to do first. I started to straighten out my desk so I could have a place to work but I stopped that because I don't have the time. Then I started to grade some papers but I can't concentrate with all this junk on my desk."

"What are you going to do then?"

"I don't know. In fact, I'm getting to hate this place and all this mess. How about going out with me for a cup of coffee?" Todd asked.

This haphazard approach, diffused energy output, inability to concentrate for very long on a task, and cluttered work environment are common symptoms. They try to tackle everything at once rather than work systematically and persistently on one, two or three projects until each is completed.

A very, very successful insurance man I know has a yearly, monthly and daily schedule. Fred knows exactly what he is going to do in the course of a work day. He knows how many people he's going to see, how much time he will spend with them, and what he hopes to accomplish. Fred is just 45 years old, but he already has a multi-million dollar insurance business.

Fred explains his attitude as this: "There are only so many hours in the day and some of this time I enjoy just relaxing. But how can you enjoy relaxation unless you have something to relax from?"

This rather interesting concept is also a valid one. Too many people think they are relaxing when they are in fact escaping. So what is called "relaxation" becomes a guilt feeling and soon there are pangs of stress and anxiety because you are watching television when you should be writing a report.

Time you could be using to get work done is spent thinking about *other* things you feel you should be doing. What happens is that these feelings are present regardless of what you are working on. Since you do not fully commit yourself emotionally or intellectually to the task, it takes considerably longer for you to complete it, if you do at all..

Your failure to set up priorities or make judgments about what has to be done first, second, third, etc., adds to your confusion. Faced with a series of tasks, you avoid the decision completely by doing something totally unrelated.

Your mind works like this: "I have a report that has to get done, I should read this journal article, I want to clean my desk, I have two projects that I should begin. What should I do first? I think I'll make a few telephone calls or go down the hall to talk to Joe." These are forms of escape which only add to the guilt you feel because you are not doing what you must do if you want to achieve. Work does not get done by dodging it.

Those who lug hefty briefcases to and from the office present a familiar example of disorganization and failure to focus. How often have you taken home work that "has to be done tonight"? But because you are so overwhelmed by the quantity of work, you don't get around to opening the briefcase. Or if you do open it, you are so confused about what is *most* important, that nothing gets done.

While your intentions may be good, for the most part the briefcase carrying becomes a ritual. And don't fool yourself that you are getting exercise. If muscles are what you're looking for, why not put barbells in the case instead of papers? That way you can get your exercise without feeling guilty because you haven't done all the assignments you promised yourself to do.

By the way, this idea is not so far fetched. One client once told me that on his way to and from the train station he would lift his case up and down fifty times with each hand. "After all," he said, "as long as I had to carry it home anyway—that's the thing to do, you know—and I rarely did much work at home, I felt I ought to get some benefit out of this ritual. I really built up my arm muscles."

What Happens When Things Don't Get Done

These problems, namely inability to figure priorities, putting assignments off, attempting to tackle too many projects at once, and thinking about what has to be done rather than doing them result in unnecessary pressures, anxieties and frustrations. One symptom of such stress is tiredness; continual headaches is still another symptom.

Underachievers are prime targets for other physiological reactions to self-imposed stress. Anxiety can result from an uneasy feeling of wanting to do something, but not knowing what to do or how to get it done.

If you want an idea of how the body reacts to lack of organization and the resulting anxiety, think of how you feel on a Sunday morning when you have nothing planned, yet you feel like doing something. You walk around the house or go outside while trying to decide what to do. Several hours may go by, but still no plan. By afternoon, you're probably exhausted from doing nothing.

Now compare that feeling to the one you get when you know precisely what you want to do and you go about doing it. During the same time interval you will feel invigorated because you have directed your pent-up energy. You feel good because you are not suppressing your need or desire to activate your body. This is not to say that relaxation is unimportant or unnecessary. It is. But to relax when your mind wants to be active has the opposite effect.

Starting and stopping a variety of tasks also creates anxiety. The brain can only take a certain amount of gear shifting. From this standpoint, the brain is not much different from a car. Starting an automobile, i.e., overcoming inertia, requires the greatest energy output. Also, when a car is in a rut, attempts to get it out result in spinning wheels which are taxing on the machine. Imagine the condition your car would be in if you did little more than start and stop it or spin its wheels. The battery would wear out quickly.

Similarly, your brain becomes tired and taxed when you mistreat it. Remember, you're not a machine. Yet you continuously start and stop because you've got so many ideas and problems on your mind that need to be taken care of all at once. You're tired because you rarely roll along in third gear. Most of the time you're either in first or spinning your brain wheels trying to figure out how to get moving.

There is still another factor that explains your tiredness. Most people tend to think more about incompleted tasks than they do about completed ones. Once a person has completed an assignment, he is done; he doesn't have to think about what he should do. But since you have many loose ends, you spend most of your mental energy worrying about all the things you haven't done. And you rarely experience a sense of becoming deeply involved in a project. In short, your lack of self-discipline and self-direction drains you.

As a result of disorganization and lack of self-discipline, one rarely feels that he is accomplishing anything. This failure contributes to anxiety, frustration and self-dislike. You develop a feeling of personal worth when you complete assignments. Even if you finish just one item, it's more satisfying than starting several jobs and having no product' to show for it.

Fear of Asking Questions

Your failure to get started on an assignment may be due to the fact that you do not clearly understand what to do or how to begin. Rather than ask questions so you can proceed with confidence, you are more likely to think and stew about the problem. But nothing gets done.

This may be what happens. Your boss assigns you a project and you attentively listen to his instructions. Thinking that
you understand what he expects, you return to your desk.
Several hours or maybe a day later you are ready to work
on it. But you have trouble starting because now you really
don't understand what your superior wants. Instead of
returning to your boss to ask whatever appropriate questions
will put you on the track, you put the project aside. When
you get back to it a week later the problem is no clearer.
And you are that much further behind in terms of time.

I asked an executive secretary who exhibited these characteristics: "Why don't you do *something* or why don't you
find out for sure what you're supposed to do?"

"I wouldn't want anyone to think I'm dumb," she replied.
"I'd rather try to figure out the problem myself. When I
can't, I put the work aside. If I do something when I'm
not sure it's right the work will be rejected."

What happens here is that not knowing what to do becomes
a good excuse for doing nothing. There is a better, more
productive and mature way of handling such a situation.
Check your understanding of the assignment before you
accept it or go to work on it. You might ask: "If I understand the project, this is what you're looking for---." If
you have to submit a written report you might want to
determine whether your boss would prefer a particular form.

In short, ask questions. No one will think less of you for
it. In fact your boss will respect you for your interest in
clearing up any uncertainty. Such preventative measures take
foresight and maturity. Remember, your superiors are interested in results. If you have to ask questions to get
results, then do it.

When You Encounter Obstacles

Anyone can sail through an assignment when there are no
roadblocks. Realistically, few projects are free of obstacles.
Whatever form these obstacles assume, whether it is need for

additional information, further research, or extending yourself in one way or another, achievers are willing to take the
time and to make the effort.

Underachievers quit. They do not go out of their way nor
do they have the patience to subject themselves to possible
humiliation in an effort to overcome barriers. So when they
encounter an obstacle, their first thought is to avoid it by
coming up with an excuse. Some excuses are fatalistic:

> "I know I can't crack the account, so why try?
> No matter what approach I would use it's not
> going to work."

> "Maybe it wasn't meant to be."

> "There are plenty of other projects, I'll get
> another chance."

Another form of retreating from barriers is to place blame
on external factors. Here are a few common excuses:

> "The territory is no good."

> "My clients are too demanding."

> "Nobody understands me."

> "The time pressures are too great to do a good
> job."

> "The conditions are poor."

> "I don't have the right equipment."

A very common excuse, and one which is often used by
housewives, is: "Even if I do well, I'm not going to be appreciated. So why bother?" The person who uses this excuse is

engaging in a form of psychological projection. What he or she is really saying is: "I'm not going to be rewarded by that person. I don't feel any better for doing it and the investment is far greater than the dividends I'm going to get out of this." So, she makes the other person the bad guy. The housewife who wants to have a part time job, but automatically assumes that her husband won't let her, is using this excuse. She tells herself that hubby is cruel, doesn't understand her and is unfeeling to her needs and desires. That's easier to believe than to look for a job and run the risk of failure.

Fear of change is another important aspect. After giving dozens of minor reasons why she couldn't get the part time job she said she wanted, Liz admitted, "I'll have to disrupt my whole program. If I really get a job, I'll have to get up in the morning—and I'm not sure I really want to do that." At least this way Liz can talk about wanting a job and her friends will say, "Gee, isn't that ambitious?"

If you want to achieve long range objectives, don't dodge obstacles. Meet them head on and kick them aside. Take whatever action is required to keep moving. Remember, nothing happens unless *you* make it happen; problems don't get resolved unless *you* resolve them; no one will come to your rescue unless *you* yell for help. How can others help if *you* don't let the appropriate people know you are having trouble? How can you achieve your goals if *you* do not take positive steps?

These rules and guidelines also apply to short range and relatively simple projects. Your tendency to minimize the importance of easy-to-do, nontime consuming activities leads to procrastination. "This is nothing. I'll take care of it later" is probably your attitude. But these little items build up and, before you know it, you have a large number of little items to do. Isn't it just as easy to take care of that little thing now? How much time will it take? Two, three, five minutes? Do it now and have it over with.

Why Put Off Until Tomorrow?

Many people rarely do what needs to be done at the time

they are faced with a specific task or problem. They continually put things off as if the problem will go away or resolve itself. Even tasks which are relatively simple to perform are put off. Aside from the pressure that postponement creates, last minute work is usually inferior to that which is done by pacing yourself. So they actually lose on two counts—they create unnecessary pressures and they do an inferior job.

There is no single explanation for this self-defeating behavior. In some instances a task is procrastinated if it is viewed as unimportant in relation to other tasks a person has to do. As one physician told me, "When I receive a reminder in the mail to renew a subscription or if my wife asks me to fix a chair that may take me only ten or fifteen minutes, I put it off. After all, it's so easy to take care of these matters; I can do them any time. The problem I run into is that these little jobs that are not particularly time consuming add up. Before I know it, there are so many of these little tasks to do that I don't know where to begin."

Achievers use a completely different line of reasoning. When faced with a chore, they estimate the amount of time it will take them to do the job and they either take care of it immediately or they enter it into their weekly "things to do" schedule. In so doing they do not feel bogged down either mentally or emotionally with many unfinished little projects.

Other reasons why projects are postponed are: 1) The things that have to be done require extensive preparation; 2) You're not sure of what to do; 3) It's a task you don't particularly enjoy doing; 4) Other matters are more appealing; and 5) You underestimate the amount of time it takes to do a job.

One way of overcoming the habit of putting off until tomorrow what you can do today is to analyze the *real* reasons for procrastinating. A dentist I know kept putting off writing a letter to his daughter who was away at college. Nick had been meaning to write her for several weeks and he was bothered by the fact that he had not done so. "I just can't seem to get around to it," Nick explained.

"Is it really that, or is it a case of not knowing what you want to say?" I asked.

Well, if you really want to know," he admitted sheepishly, "I'm not good at writing letters. I've got lots of things to tell her but I don't know where or how to begin."

"Forget about how it's written. Take a sheet of paper and jot down all the things you want to say to her."

After Nick did this, I told him to write the letter using the points he had jotted down as an outline. Within thirty minutes he had the letter completed. He felt relieved, a feeling he could have experienced three weeks prior to my encounter with him.

This approach can work for you. Just ask yourself: "Can I do this little task, which will take no more than a few minutes, *now*? If I can't do it now, why not? What's standing in my way?" Once you analyze the problem you will find yourself doing more chores now and having more time later.

Do You Magnify Anticipated Problems?

Another frequent reason why people have difficulties with long range projects is that they magnify anticipated problems long before they occur.

A 34-year-old physicist named Cliff was telling me about his difficulties in finding a new job. His approach was to either answer ads or contact employment agencies.

"How about making direct calls yourself?" I asked him.

"I couldn't do that. I'd get turned down," Cliff said.

"How do you know unless you try?"

"I just know, that's all."

While Cliff was able to find a job by employing his two techniques, his attitude (which seemed a way of life for him) affected his professional growth. Any time Cliff had to tackle a new challenge he found all sorts of reasons why he should not proceed with it. In effect Cliff was a one man hanging jury. Cliff's anticipated fears and tendencies to assume that major problems were present when they were really not prevented him from making progress as a physicist. He was constantly wondering what would happen if this or that went wrong. By the time he built his case, which was based on wrong assumptions, his minor obstacles had been magnified in his mind many times out of proportion to reality. Eventually, Cliff's self-created roadblocks paralyzed him. And, of course, he now had an excuse for not working as a physicist.

Achievers, in contrast, are aware that problems occur with any meaningful project. They even try to anticipate setbacks so they will be able to take appropriate steps to work through or around them. Achievers see little value in exaggerating or overestimating the extent of difficulty. They take problems in stride and think of ways to overcome them rather than use them as excuses for backing away from a challenge. In short, achievers see problems as opportunities to utilize their potential while underachievers view them as reasons for nonaction.

CHAPTER VII

A PLAN OF ACTION

Need for Structure

If you are disorganized to the point of not getting as many projects done as you would like, and if you lack the self-discipline to stick with a task until it is completed, you probably require greater structure. Although you may not realize it, you want to be told specifically what has to be done and when. You want someone, whether it's your boss or spouse, to make your priority and deadline decisions for you.

In short, you want and encourage others to hound you and push you to get assignments done. Unless someone is riding you and reminding you to get certain items done, you let your work and obligations slide. It is as if you need the security and comfort that comes from knowing for sure what is required of you. When someone is there to remind you what has to be done first and second, you don't have to make those decisions. And you think, "What a relief!"

But look at the trap you create for yourself. You really resent being treated like a child—yet you force others into this position. Next, most bosses neither have the time nor the patience to provide such structure. So they let you flounder and begin to view you as a hopeless case. Once this happens you can forget about raises or promotions. The net result is that your failure to structure your own time and your inability to assign priorities is viewed as immature and interferes with your development on and off the job.

This dilemma can be resolved by developing your own structure, rather than depending on others to do it for you. You can learn to be your own boss, make your own decisions as to priorities, and relieve the frustrations that come from people constantly telling you what to do.

How to Stay on Top of Things

Since being organized is a way of life, chances are that if you are disorganized at work you also exhibit this behavior at home. The way to overcome the habit is to put the following ideas into practice in both places.

Your first step is to develop two written lists of all the projects you have to do or want to get done—one list should be labeled "Things to do at work" and the other "Things to do at home." These are your master lists which should be kept up to date. As you get items on the list done, check off the completed ones and add to the list new projects you want to undertake. Also, these lists should be readily available so you can refer to them as needed.

Making written lists is extremely important for several reasons. First, the act of putting on paper what needs to be done relieves much of the "I've got so much on my mind" feeling you've been experiencing. Second, it puts the amount of work you really have to do in proper perspective. The amount of work doesn't appear quite as formidable or as insurmountable when you list exactly what needs to be done.

I recall talking with a supervisor who was upset about all the things he had to do. Jason's problem was familiar; I've heard it many times. "Just how much do you have to do?" I asked him.

"I don't know, but it's a lot," he replied.

"Write down those things you have to do."

His list consisted of five items, none of them very difficult or time consuming. When Jason looked at his list, he remarked with amazement, "I guess I made a bigger deal out of this than I should have." This realization unfroze him so that he was able to charge ahead with renewed vigor.

Another reason for putting these lists in writing is that they serve as reminders of what should be done. You don't have to depend on anyone else. Also, a list unclutters your mind. Now you can focus on the tasks at hand. And you don't have to worry about forgetting a future project.

Finally, the list has therapeutic value in that you feel a sense of accomplishment when you check off things you have completed. It's reassuring to look at your list at the end of a day and see all the projects you've actually finished. The checked off items are behind you and you don't have to think about them again. The checking off (or scratching out if you prefer) process relieves those self-deprecating feelings ("I wasted the day" or "I got little done").

Now that you've made your lists, indicate on the left side of each item the amount of time—hours, days or weeks—it will take you to complete the task. Be liberal in your time estimate. Don't fall into the trap of underestimating the amount of time it takes to get a job done.

Your next step is to assign priorities to each of the tasks you listed. Ask yourself: What is most important right now? What is the next important item on my list? Go down the list until each project has an assigned priority (1, 2, 3, 4, etc.). In the past this was difficult for you to do because you probably did not think in terms of specific jobs to do. Instead, you thought about the mass of work which needed to be done as if it all had to be completed at once.

You can't do everything at once, even if they are all important. Once you make your decisions and assign priorities you will feel relieved.

Now comes the difficult part—planning your days and weeks to accomplish those tasks you said are important. To do this you need a weekly calendar. You may purchase one or make one yourself if you like. Be sure it is small enough to carry with you.

It is best to plan your week on Sunday evening. That gets you off to a good start on Monday. Your initial step is to fill in those times which are definitely accounted for. For example, lunch time, travel time, meetings you know about in advance and other known commitments should be specified.

Then include the amount of time you wish to spend on any given project. For example, you estimate that a particular task will take you six hours to complete and you want or need to complete it in one week. You might assign two hours per day—Monday through Wednesday—for this job. Indicate on your calendar which two hours you plan to spend on that project. Do this for every item on your list. See Figure 1 for a composite illustration of how to organize for achievement.

When possible, tasks that can be accomplished in a short period of time should be completed quickly. This provides quick rewards and relieves a great deal of pressure. Answering mail and returning calls are examples of such short term tasks.

While such a planning calendar may sound like you're locking yourself into a tight schedule, this is not its purpose. It is simply intended as a guide. Circumstances may require you to alter your schedule or rebudget your time. That's all right—as long as you have some constant reminder of your obligations to yourself and others.

In addition to scheduling your days, you will also find it helpful to structure your evening work activities. Many people take work home to do in the evening. But as I pointed out earlier, because they try to do too much they wind up doing nothing. Planning on a day to day basis can resolve that problem. For example, let's say you have time to do only two hours of work from an 8 to 10 p.m. period. Take home whatever work can be done within this time. Don't stuff your briefcase full of work that obviously requires six hours of work.

By taking home only the amount of work you can do in the time you've allotted yourself, and completing it, you will feel a real sense of achievement. Isn't that more satisfying than bringing home a heavy suitcase but doing practically nothing with it because the thought of beginning paralyzes you?

FIGURE 1

HOW TO PLAN FOR ACHIEVEMENT

Things To Do	Time Required	Priorities
A	2 hrs.	2
B	10 hrs.	1
C	20 minutes	5
D	10 minutes	3
E	25 minutes	6
F	6 hrs.	4
G	4 hrs.	7
H	2 hrs.	
I	4 hrs.	

Time	Days of Week						
	Mon.	Tues.	Wed.	Thurs.	Fri.	Sat.	Sun.
AM							
9:00	C,D,E	G	F	G	B		
10:00	H				H		
11:00	A		A		F		
12:00 PM							
1:00	Lunch						
2:00	B	B	B	B	F		
3:00							
4:00	I	I					
5:00							
6:00							
7:00							

While your work calendar and list of things to do are useful tools for organizing yourself, they are not enough. In order to avoid spinning your wheels and shifting gears too often, you have to force yourself to focus on the activity listed on the calendar. You must literally push yourself, unless there is a good reason not to, to work on the specified task for the length of time you've allotted. Don't let yourself get distracted. Remember, you are more interested in getting things done than in starting a number of tasks. Quality rather than quantity should be your main concern at this stage of your development.

Planning your weeks and days, as well as listing what needs to be done in their order of importance, is particularly useful for those people employed in relatively unstructured jobs. Salesmen, executives and college professors are a few individuals who must schedule their own work and time. Because no one is there to check on them every minute they have to be their own boss.

Achievers in these nonstructured professions automatically do what I recommend, although they may not be as rigid about it. For them it is a habit to organize their time and to attend to what must be done. That is why they accomplish as much as they do.

Less compulsive people, on the other hand, have to make a conscious effort at structuring their lives. These recommended guidelines are constructive steps toward moving in that direction. I have suggested this as your initial task because it produces immediate results. You will find that the work you have to do will get done.

Need To See Immediate Fruits of Labor

A bright but unsuccessful executive once told me: "Little things of low importance are not hard to achieve, but larger objectives or gearing up for major efforts is almost impossible for me. The questions always seem to be: How do I go about it? Can I really do it? If I do it, what good will it do? Many times the answer is to stop before I really get started."

With these attitudes, it is obvious why he has difficulties working for long range goals and has problems accomplishing anything.

Admittedly, getting started is not an easy task for most people. The main reasons achievers have less difficulty in overcoming inertia are: 1) They are willing to invest the time necessary to achieve future rewards; 2) They have a plan of action for achieving their goals; 3) They know what they are doing or are supposed to be doing; 4) They do not magnify anticipated difficulties; 5) They take constructive steps to resolve problems when they occur; and 6) They are not afraid to ask questions when necessary.

Typical underachievers usually express a great deal of enthusiasm about an assigned project or task that they undertake. After all, it's fun and exciting to begin a new assignment. That feeling lasts for a few days. It dies the moment they encounter difficulties—either real or imagined. Suddenly the project becomes a major burden and they lose interest. It's no fun working on something that requires effort, concentration and presents problems that they don't know how to deal with. So instead of dealing with these problems in a mature fashion, their tendency is to give up.

Figure 2 is a graphic illustration of the problem that a long range project presents.

In our society people are valued and rewarded when they announce their intentions to pursue a project (S) and when they actually complete it (G). The rest of the time is investment or process time. This is the period when the real work is done. There are no rewards or prizes here. To put it bluntly, no employee is complimented for coming to work every day. Similarly, parents don't smile approvingly when their children practice the piano and coaches don't recommend awards to those players who come to football practice, regardless of their loyalty. Results are what get rewarded.

This problem is difficult for many underachievers to

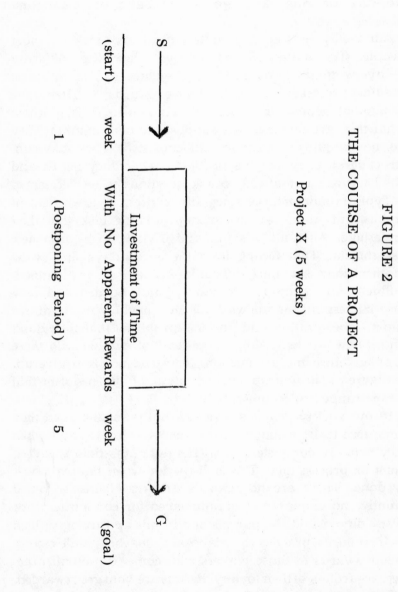

FIGURE 2

THE COURSE OF A PROJECT

Project X (5 weeks)

grasp. They need to see immediate conclusions to labor and they require regular doses of assurance that their efforts are worthwhile. Their unwillingness to *invest* unrewarded time for some uncertain future gain prevents them from directing their energies toward long range goals. They don't see it as an investment, but as a waste of energy. "Who really cares how hard I work?" is the question asked.

Because of this reasoning, their strategy is to invest as little time as possible between the start and the goal with the hope that they will be as successful as if they put in a one hundred per cent effort. Naturally, they are disappointed when their product is not well received by others. Their excuse is that they didn't have enough time. They would rather hurriedly do what they must to get by than to invest energy over a long period of time.

Their desire for quick results and personal rewards, as well as their failure to stay with a project until it is completed, is even reflected in such a relatively simple task as reading a book.

Typically, they will pick up a book which they are interested in reading and go through the following antics: 1) Leaf through the book to see how long the chapters are; 2) Look at the last page to check on the number of pages the book contains; 3) Read for about ten or fifteen minutes or maybe just think about reading it; 4) Make a judgment that there is not enough time to finish a book of that length now; and 5) Put it aside with the promise that they will get to it when there is more time. Usually they do not get to the book at all. Implicit in step 5 is the assumption that they must finish the book in one sitting. However, most people cannot finish a fairly lengthy book in one or two hours.

Still another symptom of their need for quick feedback is their tendency to turn in work quickly without checking it. To check over one's work requires extra effort and a willingness to postpone immediate pleasures for future rewards. They don't focus on a task and do it right. No, they start a new activity since that's generally more exciting than sticking with the one they have already started.

These inner thoughts and antics are major self-defeating barriers. Unable to see an immediate end project, quick rewards or recognition, they give up in desperation. This is why they have difficulties being highly productive in such fields as sales of high priced items, research, writing and consulting. The payoff in these professions comes painfully slow.

The need to see immediate results explains why they have difficulties acquiring the basic skills necessary to achieve. Their lack of patience was revealed to me by an aspiring writer who said, "I want to be an advertising copywriter but it takes too long to learn." To date he has not made a dent in pursuing a writing career.

In their eagerness to see quick results, many nonproductive people focus on the outcome or rewards without considering the means for achieving them. They think about what they want to do without planning how to do it. They dream of greatness and think about the fame they will enjoy. They become so engrossed in how it's all going to come out that they try too hard. As a result, they are tense, unable to think clearly and unable to focus their energy on realizing their dreams. More often than not, they miss the mark.

The late golf great, Tony Lema, was leading in the last tournament of his career. Approaching the seventeenth hole, he had a two stroke lead over the second place man. He bogied the final two holes and lost. When asked by a reporter what happened, Lema said, "I was thinking of my final score rather than concentrating on the hole I was playing." For that moment Tony Lema was behaving like an underachiever. He was more concerned with the final product so he failed to focus on the individual steps.

This example illustrates what I earlier referred to as the Superman complex. Underachievers like to leap tall buildings with a single bound. While the fictional man of steel could get away with it, most people must advance through steps and stages.

Contrast the Superman complex with the attitude of a colleague who has written three books. I asked Claude once, "How do you write a book? I would imagine it is a monumental task."

He replied, "I don't write books. I write chapters; most of the time I only write about a small topic. When I get through writing all I need to about a particular subject, I put it together. It's like eating a steak. You can't devour it all at once. You take small bites."

Since you need quick rewards, and because process time can be valuable and even interesting, your strategy has to be: 1) To reduce your investment time so that you receive immediate and regular rewards and 2) To maintain your enthusiasm throughout a long range project so that you can complete it. By following this plan you will be much less disgusted with yourself than you have been in the past. Your kicks will not only come at the beginning and end of a project, but at every step of the way from start to finish.

Although you may not realize it, when you shrug off process time (I call it the joys of doing) you are cheating yourself. The man who works strictly for his paycheck, which comes every week or two weeks, or the person who is biding his time until his vacation, are two examples of people who are losing out on a major portion of life, and are not enjoying the happiness of pursuit. They are just killing time and going through motions.

To overcome these difficulties and gain greater pleasure from work, you will find it helpful to divide a long range goal into meaningful sub-goals as depicted in Figure 3. This way you can accomplish several things. First, if you compare Figures 2 and 3, you will see that the distance between sub-goals is smaller than the distance between S to G in Figure 2.

This means that your investment time between rewards is reduced to a tolerable level. By making each sub-goal your target you not only see results immediately, but each

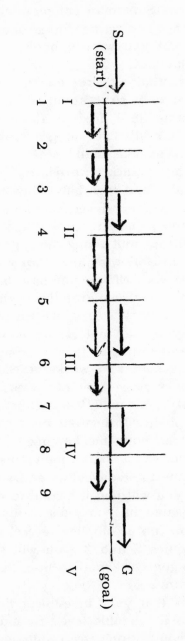

FIGURE 3

Project X (5 weeks)

Weeks I to V
S.G. (Sub-goals) 1 to 9

accomplishment will renew your vigor to continue.

A second value in establishing sub-goals is that the enthusiasm you get from each minor achievement will carry you through the entire project until it's completed. Finally, by accomplishing long range goals in this manner the end result will be much better because you will have taken the time and put forth the required effort to do the job right.

Let's apply this principle to a specific situation. Suppose one of your objectives is to read a particular book of 250 pages. Your first step is to determine approximately how many pages you can read in one hour. Then decide how many hours per week you want to devote to reading the book.

You decide that three hours a week is all you can spare. Schedule it in your calendar. Next, set your sub-goals—either one hour per sitting or "x" number of pages. Don't put down the book until you have met one of these objectives.

The good feeling that comes from setting and hitting a target will be an invigorating experience for you. More important, you know that after so many hours you will complete the book. You will not only enjoy the end result but also the process.

This approach also works effectively in preparation activities—practicing, going to school, developing an account, conducting research or working on any long term project which may not yield immediate dividends. I cannot tell you what specific sub-goals to set, but make them meaningful and personally satisfying. Remember, what you are interested in is some tangible and worthwhile guidepost that tells you when you are moving forward. If you have to, give yourself a pat on the back when you reach a sub-goal, since it is an accomplishment.

I find myself employing this strategy when I have to drive for long distances. I don't particularly enjoy driving, but the experience is less painful if I say to myself that my intermediate destination is the next town on the map. When

I reach it I feel relieved and ready to drive to the next town. All it does for me is split the trip up mentally. Hence, the total drive does not seem as long as it would be if I did not apply this technique.

Defining Your Objectives

This approach forces you to plan ahead instead of jumping in first and thinking later. When you let things happen on a day to day basis without seriously considering where your acts are leading you, each individual action is disjointed rather than tied together.

A student of mine had a project that was assigned to him a month in advance. One week before it was due Brian began to worry because he had not started the assignment. He came to me for advice and this is the conversation that followed:

"I have to write a report comparing the training approaches of several banks in the Chicago area. I thought it was an easy assignment, but when I started to think about it, it became monsterous," Brian said.

"Let's examine the elements of the problem. First, how would you go about getting the basic information you need?" I asked.

"I suppose I'd have to talk to either the personnel men or the training directors of banks."

"O.K. Write down on a piece of paper: Must talk with man in charge of training. How many banks do you wish to sample and which ones?"

"I think four is sufficient," Brian said.

"Write down the names of the banks you want to contact. When you call, what will you say to them?"

"I haven't thought about it."

"Well, let's think about it now. Write down what you will say when you call a contact."

"First I would tell him I'm a student doing this project.

Then I'd ask him if I could interview him on his approaches and views toward training. And finally, I'd arrange for an appointment."

"What questions will you ask him when you meet with him? Have you thought about that?" I asked.

"No, but I will now."

About fifteen minutes later I said, "You have eight questions, which is a good starting point. Some may occur to you when you talk to the men. Now let's talk about writing the report."

"That's easy. The questions I'll be asking will serve as the basis of my report. In fact, the whole project looks easy now."

A follow-up discussion with Brian several days later revealed that he was well on his way toward completing his assignment. His failure to dissect the problem and objectives into manageable parts created unnecessary anxiety. He exaggerated the magnitude and complexity of his assignment by not developing a step by step plan for achieving results.

This tendency is characteristic of less productive people. They tend to look at the total picture and in so doing miss the components. Naturally when a problem is viewed that way it seems hopelessly unattainable. After a while the nature of the problem becomes even fuzzier and more difficult to cope with.

Achievers, however, approach problems and long range objectives in an organized and logical manner. They rely less on inspiration and more on systematic planning. In doing so, they minimize the confusion normally associated with tackling a problem. They do not feel that they must accomplish everything at once. They first develop a plan of action and commit themselves to the long range goal.

Specifically, most achievers use the technique of asking themselves: "What are the objectives of this project? What am I trying to find out?" Answers to these questions allow them to define the activities they will be performing. They have an answer to the question: "What do I have to do to accomplish these objectives?" Once they know what they have to do, they develop a check list which they can refer to in case they go astray. When you know where you're going it's much easier to stay on the track.

Defining objectives serves another important function— it allows you to appropriately categorize the problem. It raises the question: "In what way is this similar to other problems I have faced?" By viewing a project in this way, and drawing on principles learned from similar assignments, achievers need not approach every problem as if it were unique.

Achievers next outline the specific steps required to reach each of the objectives they have set. These steps, or plans of action, allow achievers to schedule their time in relation to other work they have to do. It also provides them with a basis for scheduling any personnel they may need to help them with the project.

Third, they proceed with each step one at a time, until each objective is fulfilled. And finally, the achievers put the pieces together into a meaningful whole.

This approach for handling complex problems may be summarized as follows:

1. Why—am I doing it?

2. What—am I going to do?

3. How—will I accomplish it? (What tools or information do I need?)

4. Do it.

5. Combine the elements.

Achievers usually approach most problems this way, whether they are difficult or easy. Less productive people tend to be sloppy, careless, and not very conscientious even when they face an easy task. Because they do not realize that seemingly simple projects also require a plan of action, their projects fail to materialize more often than not.

CHAPTER VIII

WHAT DO YOU WANT TO BE
WHEN YOU GROW UP?

Do You Have a Career Roadmap?

Has this ever happened to you? You are driving in your car, in a rush to get somewhere, when suddenly it occurs to you that you may be going in the wrong direction. Rather than stop to ask for directions or look at a roadmap you keep going because you don't want to waste time. It's easier to just keep moving even though you may be going further out of your way. It's easier not to stop even though you may spend more time retracing your steps.

Or have you had this experience? You want to go somewhere by car, although you don't know specifically either where you want to go or what you want out of the trip. So you get into the car and drive. Since you don't know where you're going or what you're looking for, chances are you won't recognize a worthwhile destination or landmark along the way to a destination. Similarly, if you have no idea what you want in the way of a career, you may be passing up opportunities because you do not recognize them as such.

These two examples illustrate a self-defeating characteristic that is probably more common than any other mentioned thus far. Aimless drifting, failure to take stock of who you are, and to define where you are going and work out a roadmap for getting there, are sources of constant frustration. You are essentially running a race with no destination. How can you put forth your best effort when you don't know what your target is? How can you invest effort in a job which you are not sure is really for you?

> "I often feel like I'm in a sea of despair with no landmarks or points of reference to guide me."

> "If you can imagine yourself in the middle of a lake with no sign of an end point, then you know how I feel."

> "In all of my years above the age of ten I have never been able to truly define where I'm going or what I want to do with my life. I have dreams of achieving greatness, but that's where they end—as dreams."

These expressions of hopelessness and helplessness are symptoms of a more basic difficulty discussed earlier: failure to focus on a problem and to develop an appropriate plan for resolving it. Many people neither seriously think about their career objectives nor do they develop a strategy for achieving whatever objectives they have set. But, they make halfhearted attempts at a variety of jobs. They'll go in one direction, then another one, and when they are dissatisfied, they'll just look for something else. By the time they reach their forties they have tried a half-dozen careers part way. There is no evidence of a pattern either, because they have never thought through what they really want out of life.

While you are going to school it is reasonable, and even expected, not to know what you want to be when you grow up. But, there comes a time when you should have some idea what road you want to travel. It is no longer appropriate to drift, taking each day as it comes and hoping for some opportunity to come your way. It won't. You have to make your own opportunities. Opportunity knocks frequently, sometimes softly and subtly. But before you can respond you must know what you want. You must be sensitive to yourself—your interests, abilities and goals.

Most underachievers dodge or gloss over the problem. When they are asked what they want in the way of a career they come up with generalizations which are meaningless. Many I have talked with say: "I want a responsible job" or "I want to work with people" or "I want a job that will give me a challenge."

But these wants can be satisfied by almost any position or job. For example, a railroad conductor's job fits these criteria. Also cab drivers, secretaries, professors, lawyers, physicians and janitors' jobs are responsible, challenging and allow them to work with people. These generalizations are convenient ways of avoiding the difficult task of being specific in your analysis.

I am not suggesting that you have to know exactly what you're going to do five, ten or fifteen years from now. Many men have three or four careers in their lifetime. When they've succeeded in one, and it no longer offers a challenge, they may decide to move in a different direction. However, this new direction is generally related to or an extension of their last career.

I know a man who began his career as a school teacher. After seven years of teaching, and after passing the appropriate exam, he became a school principal—an administrative function. His interest in television as an educational medium prompted him to find opportunities in this area. Because of his excellence as a television teacher, he was offered an opportunity to develop and produce other courses for television. In effect, he went through several stages in which he progressed from teacher to educational television producer.

This is not an unusual situation; many cases could be cited of people changing fields. However, each new field is a natural extension of the old and it grows out of a sincere interest to expand horizons. It follows a pattern.

Developing career plans requires certain steps. The approach I will describe has been useful to others. Try it. You may find that you are in the wrong field, and consequently are not achieving what you want to achieve.

Inventory Your Interests

Every job requires you to make certain compromises. Most positions have about five elements or dimensions which are crucial, daily aspects of the job. Now you may dislike one or two of these elements. If you focus on the two dimensions that you dislike and allow this to affect your total performance, you'll fall down on the job.

An electrician I saw recently has this problem. Bruce said that there are times on the job which are terribly unchallenging, like those spent putting up fixtures. What is challenging about his job, he told me, is rewiring a house. Changing a fixture is nothing.

Said Bruce, "I'll look at that fixture and I'll play with it. And before I know it, I'll have spent four hours changing a fixture which should have taken me only fifteen minutes. I wind up saying, 'Boy, isn't this job dull!'"

Bruce's *job* wasn't dull. He made it dull because he expanded the dullness to hours when it could have been done in minutes. If you expand the dullness, the negative aspects of your job will overshadow the positive ones. And you are making a prophecy come true. Your prediction may be that the job is not right for you. So you gather all kinds of evidence and even perform in a negative, dull way to fulfill your prophecy. You also make compromises with yourself, and you remain with any job, however boring it may be. The net result is that you mark time at work rather than produce.

Your aim ought to be to obtain a job or follow a career in which you have to make the fewest number of compromises. The more compromises you make the greater your dissatisfaction will be. If you want to determine what career is best suited to your likes and dislikes, here's a way to go about taking an inventory of the situation.

Your first task is to think back to all the jobs you've ever had and write down on a sheet of paper all the things you really enjoyed doing in each of these jobs. That is, what aspects of these jobs were really satisfying to you and gave you the greatest kicks?

On another sheet of paper list those tasks which you have found distasteful. Describe them in detail. Take your time in developing the two lists. You probably won't be able to do it in one sitting. Soul searching requires time and patience.

As a guideline for preparing your list, Look at Figure 4 which shows the likes and dislikes of a purchasing agent who was unhappy and unsuccessful in his work. He later found a job as a claims adjuster, a position he found much more appealing.

Now that you have developed your own list of what you liked and disliked about your past jobs, itemize on another sheet of paper those things you enjoy doing in your spare time at home. These may be hobbies or other interests. There is no rule which states that a paying job has to be inconsistent with your off-the-job interests.

While you may want to keep your home interests separate from your work activities, this home list will sharpen your focus on the kind of work and activities which appeal to you. You will be able to see more clearly how you want to earn your living because you are forcing yourself to examine your interests objectively (probably for the first time in your life).

Published vocational interest inventories may be helpful in defining your interests. But, chances are, they will not reveal anything more about yourself than you already know. After all, who knows better than you what you enjoy or do not enjoy doing?

Another useful approach to examining your interests is to ask yourself: "What would I like to do with my time if

FIGURE 4

Inventory of Likes and Dislikes as Prepared by a Purchasing Agent Who Did Not Like His Job.

Likes:

1. Meeting people. I find people interesting and enjoy being with them.

2. I like to buy goods, particularly if I have to spend other people's money.

3. I like talking to people on the phone or in person.

4. I like to deal with *broad* problems.

5. I want to be of service to others; I want to feel I'm helpful to people.

6. I prefer working on the outside most of the time rather than being tied to a desk.

7. I like working with numbers—figuring details out mathematically—nothing complicated, however.

8. I like a job where I have an understanding supervisor who is available to answer questions.

9. I want a job in which I know where I stand at all times. I want a boss who will tell and discuss with me what I'm doing right and wrong.

Dislikes:

1. I don't like to be inside or to sit at a desk all day.

2. I don't like bargaining with people about prices.

3. I don't like to make important decisions.

4. I don't like too many pressures or a lot of people making demands on me all at once.

5. I don't like to be rushed.

6. I don't like a job where I have to say "no" to people.

7. I don't like a lot of detail work.

I were independently wealthy?" Your answer to this question may draw attention to possibilities you have discounted in the past because you were not able to visualize means for realizing these dreams.

One man who felt boxed in by a desk job he did not like told me that if he were independently wealthy he would like to travel extensively. This was not a whim. Andy really would have liked this as a way of life if he could afford it. At my suggestion, he investigated and later accepted a position with an airline. While Andy was not overly enthused with his new job (a compromise he willingly made), he was able to travel at a substantial cost savings.

What Abilities Do You Have?

Your next step is to inventory your abilities and skills. Here again, you do not need formal tests to tell you what you are or are not capable of doing. With some honest effort you can analyze yourself. To start with, here are a list of questions and factors to consider which should be helpful to you.

1. What is your intellectual potential—superior, well above average, above average or average? You've had enough experience to make this judgment. You know whether or not things come easy to you or whether you have to work particularly hard before you understand what is going on. Are you quick or slow to pick up ideas?

2. Do you work better with ideas (i.e., intangibles) or with concrete details? If you work better with ideas, you probably can express yourself well orally or in writing. If you work better with tangible objects, you probably would feel more comfortable with a job in which you could see, feel, touch and/or taste the product you are dealing with. People who deal with ideas may also work with facts and figures, but for them these tangibles are used to support ideas and concepts.

3. Do you have mechanical ability? If you enjoy (and do a good job at) fixing objects, if you can envision items from a three dimensional viewpoint or if you are able to take clocks apart and know where the pieces fit, you may have some mechanical aptitude.

4. How good are you with clerical and other details? Are you accurate? If you do a decent job of keeping records and maintain some semblance of order in your home and at work, it's likely that you are sufficiently detail minded to perform normal administrative or office functions. If details bore you and you are not an orderly person by nature, avoid jobs that require this ability.

5. How do you get along with people? Do you work better by yourself or with others? Do people consider you easy or difficult to talk to? Can you approach others with ease or do you feel embarrassed or self-conscious about it?

6. Are you a good planner or are you better at implementing or doing jobs which are spelled out for you? Some people are better doers than planners, while others may do an excellent job of planning but do not have what it takes to put these plans into action.

These are just a few of the questions which will help you gain a fairly good picture of your skills. It may be that some of these abilities are not as well developed as you would like them to be. You may be lacking abilities that are required for the type of career you want. If so, certain skills such as planning, getting along with people and self-expression (either oral or written) can be developed through additional training. Universities and local high schools offer courses in these areas.

Other Factors to Consider

Knowing your interests and abilities will give you a good start in planning your career. However, there is one more thing you must do to complete this picture of yourself. You have to detail the conditions under which you would like to work. To a large degree your success in thinking through this question will depend upon how well you know yourself as a person. Your personality makeup has a great deal to do with the types of jobs or careers that are most suitable for you.

Here are just a few questions you might consider:

1. To what degree can you take frustrations, such as frequent disappointment or rejection?

2. How independent are you? Can you function well without much supervision or do you need constant guidance and direction from supervisors?

3. How aggressive are you? Are you an initiator or a follower?

4. How adaptable or flexible are you? Can you roll with the punches or do you work better under routine conditions?

5. How well can you handle time pressures?

6. How do you feel about traveling? How much travel can you handle? Are you emotionally equipped to do it?

7. To what degree can you tolerate putting in time on work, with no immediate results?

Other questions about your temperament and emotional

stability will occur to you as you think about yourself. Consider them carefully.

Your purpose in examining your interests, abilities and personality characteristics is twofold. First, there are few things more important to a person than his career. People like to feel important and to have a sense of purposefulness. The right occupation can either do this for a person or it can deny him of such pleasures. Dr. Karl Menninger once said that better than seventy per cent of the men in mental institutions have had serious career problems. They didn't like what they were doing. This is also a major source of women's frustrations and personal difficulties. You can avoid such problems.

Second, by pinpointing what you enjoy doing, the conditions under which you enjoy doing them, and the skills available to you, you can search for positions which will have real meaning to you. If you have developed the inventories which were discussed earlier, either by yourself or with the help of a trained person, you have before you the tools to make realistic, appropriate career decisions.

Your next step is to implement these decisions either immediately or at some future date. Specifically, you may want to look for a position that is more suitable to you. Or, if other positions—promotions or transfers—arise within the organization where you are currently employed, you can evaluate their merits in terms of your needs. Don't fall into the trap of accepting a promotion just because it is offered, or a higher paying job because the salary is attractive.

A case in point involved an excellent foreman who was promoted to a supervisor. Following the promotion Lee's efficiency dropped substantially. He complained of not sleeping at night and an intense dislike for his new job. Lee knew in advance that he was ill-equipped for the new position but he did not have the courage to admit this to his boss. Nor did he want to be demoted, since it would be humiliating. Lee lived with his misery until finally he was fired for "not utilizing his potential."

The Underachieving Housewife

There's no question in my mind that many housewives are underachievers and are unhappy. Let's take a look at a typical housewife who spends seven days a week with a bunch of "babbling kids" with whom she can't communicate. All she can do is holler at them. She feeds them, changes them, comforts them. No wonder she gets just plain tired.

If our average housewife doesn't have a husband who understands and supports her efforts, she feels trapped. If hubby doesn't say, "Let's do something together. Let's you and I talk without the kids around"—she looks for escape. Many dismiss their family, usually unconsciously, by getting sick. "If I'm sick," they reason, "then nobody can blame me for not doing the wash, the ironing, the dinner. I can not do what I am expected to do and not feel guilty about it." Hypochondria, although it sometimes develops into a real physical sickness, becomes an escape for many.

These are very definite pressures that will cause the symptoms of illness in a housewife—a feeling of worthlessness, a feeling of not being cared for, a belief that there's no point or purpose in life.

I ask women who are depressed and unhappy with being housewives, "Why don't you do something with your time? Why not join a group or become a volunteer?" When they respond that they can't afford a housekeeper or babysitter, I suggest that they get a job. I tell them a job will pay for a babysitter—and to remember that it's not the money that's important. It's the fact that you are getting out of the house. Then of course we get the old excuses, which are mainly based on fear of change. Housewives typically have a very basic conflict between what they want to do and what they think they can do.

I counseled one woman who had four children and was

getting a divorce. Ginny told me, "I don't know what I'm going to do. I haven't worked in fifteen years. I don't know how I'm going to support myself. And I really don't like staying at home."

"What did you do before you got married?" I asked her.

"I did some consumer and market research. I really enjoyed it."

I asked Ginny to write a resume. She gave the rather feeble excuse that she didn't know how to write one. I said to just put down what she thought was important. Well, Ginny wrote a magnificent summary of her job experience; her writing skills were outstanding. I called her and suggested how to proceed and gave her the names of various people to contact.

When I heard from Ginny a few weeks later she had received three job offers, each one higher than the one preceding. The lowest paying job was $8,500 a year. She was ecstatic, amazed that anybody would want her.

"They don't want you, they want your talent. Apparently you have some," I told her.

Ginny had had a marriage situation where her husband did not provide her with any encouragement or confidence. Despite her talents and advanced education, Ginny allowed her husband to undermine her abilities and desire to achieve. It boiled down to a situation where Ginny was fulfilling his prophecy of her. She thought: "My spouse says I'm no good. So I'll prove it." It took Ginny fifteen years to learn that you can prove anything you want to; you can prove negatively as well as positively.

Another woman I know, who was depressed, had never worked in the business world. I asked Mary to think of her talents and she told me that she considered herself an excellent seamstress because she makes beautiful clothes for the family. After some investigation, Mary started sewing and knitting class in her home and she's doing well financially.

Said Mary, "If I had only thought of this before. I wouldn't have felt like such a nothing. I've always felt I was a worthless person. Yet, I could have raised my family and still had some additional sense of accomplishment."

There are a number of ways a woman can reinforce her feeling of worth. Often a homemaking type of skill can be utilized while still being primarily a housewife. Jayne was an excellent gourmet cook who also knew how to make unusual Christmas tree decorations. Right before Christmas she put an ad in her local paper saying that she could teach people how to make decorations in her home. A number of women responded to the ad and Jayne made quite a bit of money. Now she's making arrangements to have a gourmet cooking class in her home.

Since Jayne realizes she has the potential to support herself if necessary, she is a much happier wife. Before this she was all wrapped up in an "I am a lowly housewife and that's my only mission in life" feeling.

Sometimes, a woman who is encouraged by her husband to have a career outside the home will use pregnancy as her excuse. Take Rita for example. She met her husband Chris when they were graduate students in journalism. They got married the day after graduation and friends assumed that they would both be journalists. But Rita got pregnant and immediately quit her job as asistant editor at a small magazine. She had two children within six years and seemed very happy about being a devoted wife and mother. Occasionally she would talk wistfully about the career she could have had.

After the children were older, Chris suggested that Rita go back to work. "You've got more talent than most of the writers who come into my office asking for work," he told Rita. "Why don't you put some of your skills to use."

Instead of leaping at the opportunity, Rita became very despondent. She began to cry a lot and became lethargic. Her numerous projects, all too often superficial ones, were abandoned. Then one day she told Chris that she couldn't possibly work; she was pregnant again.

Women's liberation advocates would accuse Rita of copping out. As for that movement, it's led by achievement oriented women who have suddenly rebelled at having been underachieving housewives all these years. Their concept of people doing their thing and not wasting their talents is valid.

Some of their ideas are important. The women's lib group is saying, "Look, we're not dummies. While there are some women who enjoy being housewives, there are some of us who would like to experience more. There are some of us who would like to have the opportunity to overcome obstacles other than domestic obstructions. There are some of us who would like to utilize our other talents."

Of course all female underachievers aren't women's lib advocates. Many are like Terry, who is a 33 year old college graduate, and a divorcee with two children. She needed to work, but was restricted by her motherly responsibilities. She is extremely bright and has worked in the past as a legal secretary. Yet, despite her abilities, she has not done much to use her skills since her divorce. Terry described her mother as a very dominating and overbearing woman who constantly embarrassed her as a youngster. Her mother, according to Terry, was a "know-it-all who ran everyone, including my father." Although Terry wanted to go to law school, her mother said no, adding that she thought her daughter was not bright enough. Unfortunately, the father was so easygoing that he rarely came to Terry's rescue. As a result of this background she developed an attitude that she could never do anything right.

When asked to describe the qualities she liked and disliked about herself Terry indicated that her best points were that she was affectionate, friendly, honest and sentimental. These are all traits which she feels enable her to gain other people's approval.

As for the qualities she disliked about herself, Terry said she held grudges and was shy. She is a woman who, when disappointed or upset by others, holds it in rather than confronting them with her complaint. Terry is afraid of arguments because they might hurt other people. So I inquired, "Aren't you a person? Don't you count?"

She replied, "Apparently not."

As a result of not expressing her anger, Terry has colitis, an ulcer and other minor psychosomatic disorders.

She also described herself as impatient for results, a trait that she dislikes. Terry needs rewards immediately and is not willing to make any investments in long term goals. She is easily bored and indicated that she makes no effort to think about what she wants out of life. Terry has been hoping for a magical solution to her problems.

I suggested to her that since she is an excellent secretary she ought to plan a way to obtain work at home by offering her typing and secretarial services to local businesses. We developed a program for doing this and she now has three clients for whom she works. Terry is much happier because life is not as boring as it has been. By being productive, and having additional income, she has developed a sense of self-worth and independence.

Many underachieving women develop the rather narrow belief that "what others think of my work is generally more important to me than what I think of it." One very bright woman I'm counseling revealed that she wanted to move into a management position at work, but was discouraged by her boss. When Poppy told her boss that she would like to take business courses to prepare herself for an administrative position, her boss said, "You don't need it to do a good job in this position; don't bother."

As was to be expected, Poppy did not pursue her wishes. She didn't realize that even though her boss didn't consider it important, she would have to make her own development a selfish consideration. She should take courses that will benefit her career whether or not it means anything to her boss. Poppy now sees that her boss was simply protecting his own interests. That is, if the boss discourages professional growth he will assure himself of an employee who will remain loyal to the company. Poppy certainly wouldn't look for an advanced position elsewhere unless she felt prepared. Because Poppy placed too much emphasis on her superior's opinion, she was the one who lost professionally.

CHAPTER IX

ORGANIZATIONS THAT BREED UNDERACHIEVEMENT

Highly paternalistic and loosely managed organizations or departments breed and foster underachievement—both the situational and chronic type. Universities, government and social agencies, banks and insurance companies are just a few of the operations which are a mecca for underachievers. This is not to say that all those who work for such organizations deserve that label. Nor do I mean to imply that all such organizations foster incompetence. All I am saying is that these kinds of companies and agencies share a basic personality, set of values and atmosphere which allows insecure and less productive people to remain on the payroll amost indefinitely.

Here are just two of many examples I can cite. The first involves a professor who had been with a university for 22 years. Ruben received tenure after being on the faculty for fifteen years. This meant that he could not be fired unless he committed a crime. After receiving this badge of distinction, which is also the ultimate in security, Ruben began to slack off. He stopped writing and did not keep up with his field. His interest in teaching also died. When I met him (he was one of my professors) his notes were so old that the paper was yellow from age. His students gained little, if anything, from his classes.

Despite numerous complaints against him, the administration could do nothing to get Ruben off his potential.

When they realized he was a serious detriment to the department in which he taught, the administrators tried several devious methods to force him to resign.

Their first approach was to assign him basic courses. Up to this point Ruben had been teaching graduate courses only. The chairman of the department thought that by giving Ruben basic courses to teach he would quit in anger. He did not. The following year Ruben was given just one basic course to teach, but on Saturdays. Again, he did not get the message.

When these two tactics failed, the chairman thought he would shame Ruben into quitting by not giving him any courses to teach. That is, Ruben received his full salary, which his tenure guaranteed, but he had to do nothing to earn it. At the same time the department told him that because of his unique position he did not need a secretary or office and took them away from him. He agreed, still not realizing that the administrators were trying to tell him (in not very subtle ways) that they were unhappy with him.

Having failed again, the administration's final tactic was not to invite Ruben to departmental meetings. When he questioned the chairman about this oversight, he was told that there was no real reason to invite him since he probably had nothing worthwhile to contribute. This action so infuriated Ruben that he resigned.

The real tragedy of this incident was that the professor was totally unaware of the reasons for his being mistreated. No one ever told him. No one in the administration had the courage to tell him that he was not fulfilling his obligations as a professor. He was allowed to hang himself. That was easier than taking the risk of hurting his feelings.

Another example involves a man who worked in a very large pharmaceutical firm. Bright as he was, Kevin dissipated his time and was not producing. The firm, which prided itself on being paternalistic and which had a practice of not firing anyone, paid no attention to him. They allowed Kevin to go about his business and made no demands on him. Nor did they confront him with the fact that he was not meeting their expectations.

In the absence of proper direction and the firm's failure to take active steps to get him off his potential, Kevin became very apathetic toward his job. To complicate matters, he was given regular increases in salary because it was the policy of the firm to do so. In short, the only tangible evidence Kevin had that his performance was less than satisfactory was that he was not given a promotion during his five years of employment.

During his sixth year with the firm he decided to quit for a more challenging position. Kevin had simply become disgruntled with this company's lack of guidance and overindulgence. The firm could have developed Kevin into a productive worker had they not been so concerned with paternalism. Instead, they lost him.

These examples clearly demonstrate paternalism at its worst. However, I don't believe that paternalism should be abolished or that it should not be practiced. However, it should be redefined. A concerned parent does not allow his children to do as they please; nor does he give his children all the comforts of life without expecting anything in return. He is also not so overprotective that he cripples initiative.

Similarly, organizations that wish to or need to be paternalistic cannot and should not turn their backs on incompetence if they are truly interested in their employees. To do so is to fail in their responsibilities to their employees as well as to the organization itself.

Because many organizations are not fully aware of the factors that breed underachievement, let's examine some of the characteristics. I'll also provide suggestions for change.

Too Much Security

One of our basic needs is to feel secure in our jobs. You can work more effectively if you know that you have a place to work tomorrow, next month and the month after that. If people don't feel threatened about losing their jobs, then they can attend to their work. Failure of companies to provide some security places a burden on employees which is certain to interfere with their productivity.

An equally debilitating problem which paternalistic organizations create is offering too much security. When a person knows that regardless of what he does or does not do, his job is not in jeopardy, where is the incentive to achieve? The fact is that too much security encourages workers to take their jobs for granted. Such an attitude results in laziness and sloppiness in one's work. "If nothing can happen to me, then I can get away with anything," underachievers reason.

It is this type of reasoning which is encouraged by tenure, "do not fire employees" attitudes, and other unreasonable "protect-the-employee-at-all-costs" types of policies. Such protection easily can be taken as a carte blanche for doing the minimum to get by. Thus, too much comfort discourages motivation; under such conditions it is easy to settle into a pattern of taking the easy way out.

I would encourage organizations with such policies to change them if they truly want to serve the best interests of their employees. I would do away with the tenure concept in universities and similar concepts in government agencies or profit making organizations. These policies might be changed to read: "Your job is secure as long as you perform at a level that is expected of you." Employees should not be allowed to believe they can't be discharged ever. But to enforce these changes it is necessary to establish other rules, policies and organizational structures which would modify the traditional paternalistic concept.

Loosely Managed Organizations

One reason why people feel they can simply get by in these paternalistic organizations is that standards are not established. Employees do not know what is expected of them. Objectives are not set and controls are not established for determining whether or not a person is doing his job.

In the absence of structure, personnel wander about not knowing from one day to the next what they are really supposed to do or how they are being measured. Establishing proper controls does not mean maintaining constant vigilence over workers. What it does mean, however, is that employees should understand that their performance will be reviewed, and that the quality and quantity of their output matters to their superiors. In short, employees should be led to believe that they are accountable to someone and that they are not totally independent.

Similarly, by stating expectations either in writing or orally, employees have guidelines for determining for themselves whether or not they are meeting their obligations. It is not uncommon for employees in many paternalistic organizations to readily admit that no one has told them what their job is and how they are being measured. Is it any wonder that people who are inclined to underachieve are encouraged to do so in such a loose environment?

Individuals who want to get off their potential and who are working in a loosely managed organization would do well to take the initiative despite their organization's lack of structure. You could pressure your superiors to tell you what they expect from you and how you will be judged. If you must, pressure them into telling you how they know if you are doing a good or poor job.

Admittedly, such action takes courage. You may even decide to leave a highly secure but personally frustrating position for a more challenging one. But the question you must ask yourself is this: What do I want, security with limited or no growth, or a possibly less secure job with the opportunity to use my potential?

Overprotective Organizations

In their desire not to offend their employees, "paternalistic" organizations choose to say nothing to their nonproductive workers. They prefer to be overpolite rather than confront these employees with constructive criticism and guidance aimed at improving their performance.

The company's assumption is that it is better to say nothing than to risk hurting the employee. However, such action is not only unfair to the employee because he is constantly in the dark, but it does not benefit the firm. How can a person improve when no one tells him what he is doing wrong and what he should do to change?

A bank vice-president once told me that he does not like to confront poor performing employees with honest criticism because it is not in keeping with the fatherly image of the bank. This attitude is obviously a distorted view of a benevolent father or paternalistic organization.

True paternalism, as opposed to the phony type, demands honest criticism, direction as needed and disapproval of inappropriate action. Failure to take such action is to display total lack of concern. I recall a 9 year old boy telling me that his father did not like him. When I asked him why he felt this way, he said, "Because he never spanks me." In his own way the child was saying that since his father doesn't disapprove of even naughty behavior, he probably does not care for his son.

I have heard similar comments from adults who are employed by so called paternalistic organizations. They say such things as: "No one really cares what I do," or "You can get away with almost anything here," or "They give you almost anything you need and want except personal attention." Do these comments reflect healthy paternalism?

People want to be evaluated. They want to know where they stand. An organization and its management representatives can do this without offending their employees. It is not only possible but also advisable to assess employees' performance and provide them with whatever direction or guidance they may need to improve.

Lack of Trust

Earlier I said that the looseness of many paternalistic organizations stifles personal growth for certain people. While such firms lack controls with regard to minor day to day work, they exercise very tight control when it comes to important matters. This isn't as contradictory as it might seem.

Most employees of such organizations are not allowed to make important decisions or to make judgments on matters of significance without obtaining permission from higher level personnel. Most of the time, they are discouraged from taking initiative on anything short of routine problems. Such organizations are saying to their employees, "We do not trust you." This lack of trust stifles any creativity and fosters dependency.

This type of action on the part of paternalistic companies is similar to that of the overprotective parents. Employees of these firms learn to distrust their own judgment and become passive toward their job. They learn that lack of initiative and indecision are rewarded while creativity and aggressiveness are discouraged and disapproved.

The obvious solution is that employees should be allowed to develop their ideas. They should be encouraged to exercise initiative. A policy like this places a burden on top management in that they must monitor and maintain some control over intellectually aggressive actions. But in return, such organizations develop people who are excited, not apathetic, about their jobs. They learn to trust themselves and, in the process, mature as individuals and as employees. Increased contributions to the organization will follow when employees feel that creative behavior is rewarded.

Managing Underachievers

If you are supervising an underachiever, you are probably baffled. Your first assumption is that he is lazy and does not care about his work. His reluctance or failure to come to you for help strengthens your conviction that he is not motivated to succeed. Since this attitude has to be reflected in your actions, it is likely that your impatience creates a wider gulf between you and him. Therefore, if you are like many supervisors, you take the only step you can— you consider firing him.

Actually, there are other alternatives you ought to think about before taking such a drastic and costly step (it is costly because you lose whatever investment you have in him and it is expensive to replace an employee). First, because these individuals are sensitive to criticism and they do not readily admit to weaknesses, a direct but soft spoken approach is generally well received. You might say: "It seems you have run into a problem. May I help you with it?" By offering help you are indicating that you understand him.

Attacks on this employee's ability in the form of such statements as "Why aren't you moving faster on your assignment?" or "How come you're not doing anything?" are certain to result in either a fast shuffle, an empty promise that it will get done or some other nonaction maneuver. Having bought additional time, they will continue to be nonproductive.

Another alternative is to help them plan their work. Provide them with the structure they need to function effectively. Spell out what you want them to do and meet with them regularly to see that they are doing the job. This takes time, but eventually they will learn to be more independent. This small investment of time can result in well paying dividends.

Next, give your employees constant reassurance and individual attention. Remember their famished egos. They need to know that you truly care and that their efforts are appreciated. Make them feel that they are special. It might even be worthwhile to assign them a "big brother" who, in your absence, gives them the encouragement they need.

Finally, be firm in your demands. If they feel you are a soft touch, they will take advantage of you. Adopt a philosophy of being firm but fair and understanding.

Does it pay to extend yourself on their behalf? If it is worth polishing a rough diamond, it also pays to work with an underachiever. Creative and professional managers recognize the value of developing potential talent.

CHAPTER X

OUTLOOK FOR THE FUTURE

The Enemy Within

The tendencies toward underachievement are always there. Consequently, you must be consciously aware of the pitfalls and symptoms I talked about earlier and fight them when they appear. If you are tempted to procrastinate, think about the consequences. Force yourself to do things now. It is so easy to slip back; you can't afford the luxury of easing up on your program to become an achiever.

Similarly, if you see yourself losing enthusiasm for your work or being overly sensitive to what others say, think about the causes of your feelings and take appropriate action! Seek the help of others who are interested in your well-being. Don't allow yourself to brood about your problems. You now have a foundation for directing your energies in a positive direction. Use this knowledge to your advantage.

Assuming that you do change your habit patterns from self-defeating to self-propelling, you will be pleased with the change in yourself. Most new achievers I have talked with discover a world they have never known before, after they decide to activate their potential. A recent patient said it best: "I have a hold of some processes that will allow me to work through problems. Knowing that I have these devices which work, relaxes me. I have a feeling of control.

I am operating myself rather than being bumped around by bosses, my spouse, deadlines, neighbors or friends."

One new attitude you will develop may be compared to a hungry man who is introduced to a table full of food. His tendency is to stuff himself. So it is with new achievers who realize what they have been missing. They want to catch up. They want to experience all the intellectual and cultural pleasures which they have denied themselves in the past.

There is no substitute for the joy of achievement—for getting things done and making things happen. There is no greater happiness than guiding your own future. Admittedly, your responsibilities to yourself and others increase as you elevate your standards. The more you accomplish, the more you will expect of yourself. You don't have time to feel sorry for yourself or to spend too much time rejoicing over a single accomplishment. There are always new challenges and opportunities waiting for you.

Summary of Principles

Your decision to be an achiever is, in essence, a silent contract you must make with yourself. To aid you in maintaining this commitment so that you can make things happen, I have summarized the basic principles contained in this book. Refer to them regularly.

1. Develop a sense of pride in your work or any project you undertake. Remember: When you do the best job you know how, you feel better for it and will be rewarded. Conversely, if you do poorly *you* will suffer the consequences. *You* are the one who benefits or loses by your peformance.

2. Begin to like yourself. You can do this by doing things that will allow you to pat yourself on the back.

3. Don't be self-deprecating. Nobody appreciates anyone who continually knocks himself. Furthermore, presenting

a weak front does not excuse your mediocre performance. All such action tells others is that you cannot be depended upon to follow through with your promises.

4. You don't have to be perfect. Remember: It is better to be in the race, even if you come in last, than not to be in the race at all. Adjust your objectives to a level you can reach, and then go to it.

5. Fear of failure is paralyzing. Unless you take risks, even though you may fail, you avoid the possibility of succeeding. When you are criticized, view it as a learning experience rather than a personal attack. If you assume that you will fail, you will; if you assume that "nothing ventured nothing gained," you will approach new situations with confidence. Even if you fail, the experience will have been worthwhile.

6. Don't be afraid of success. Although succeeding means greater responsibility to yourself and others, as well as pressures to maintain a high standard, aren't the benefits you gain from such efforts greater than the pressures you anticipate? If you like what you are doing, you owe it to yourself to do more of it and the best job you can.

7. Take your successes in stride. While it is all right to take pride in small accomplishments, don't blow them out of proportion. Rather, use your small successes as fuel to keep going and as incentive to meet new challenges.

8. When tackling a long range project, ask yourself: What are my objectives. Then develop a plan of action and outline the steps you need to take to get where you want to go.

9. In maintaining your interest on long range projects it will be helpful to you if you divide the project into meaningful sub-goals. In so doing you will receive relatively

quick results from your efforts while working toward the larger goal.

10. Don't focus your attention on the outcome. Results *will* come if you direct your energies on each step, one at a time. Make each step important, and you will achieve your ultimate objectives as well as the rewards that come from the achievement.

11. To organize yourself: 1) develop a things to do list and keep it up to date, 2) develop priorities and a schedule for working on each task, 3) work at one thing at a time for a significant period of time— don't jump from one task to another, and 4) plan ahead; calendars are worthwhile means for organizing your work week.

12. Pursue fewer activities and become proficient at them, rather than try to tackle a number of tasks without completing them. Also, it takes time to accomplish anything worthwhile. Superman may be able to leap tall buildings in a single bound, but humans have to work at achieving their objectives. You achieve by taking one step at a time.

13. If you encounter obstacles when working on a project, do not put the work aside. Rather, make an effort to obtain the information or material you need to complete it. Don't allow obstacles to become an excuse for not achieving.

14. Personal satisfaction does not come from dreaming or talking about accomplishments. If you use your energy to talk about the things you are going to do, there is little left for activating your ideas.

15. Do not magnify anticipated problems. Take problems in stride and think of ways of overcoming them—one step at a time.

16. It is healthier to vent your feelings than to hold them in. So what if others disapprove. What is the worst thing that can happen? How bad is it?

17. Whenever you do something that you believe is worthy of praise, congratulate yourself. Self-endorsement is much more dependable than seeking approval from others.

18. Don't be a victim of the "should complex." Take responsibility for your own decisions rather than use others as a scapegoat for actions which are distasteful to you. Make your actions, desires and words a harmonious unit rather than creating conflicts between them.

19. Don't *impose* your help on others. You may offer it, but give others the option of rejecting or accepting your offer. If you don't make your desire to be liked obvious, you will make more friends and acquaintances.

20. Be honest with yourself. If you do not like, approve of, or are not able to do what you are supposed to, make it known to those who can help you.

21. Complaining about your problems serves no constructive purpose. It may get you attention but not respect. Next time someone asks you, "how are you?" simply say, "I'm fine." You'll save considerable energy that could be directed toward productive action.

22. Refuse requests you cannot fulfill and avoid making promises you cannot keep. You can be liked and respected without sacrificing your self-esteem, basic values and integrity. Don't hurt yourself in an effort to please others. Remember, you have to like yourself first before anyone else will.

23. Inventory your interests, abilities and personal qualities for living a better life.

24. Obtain the necessary training and education to do your job better.